Log Cabin Flower Quilts

by Nancy Brenan Daniel

Bobbie Matela, Managing Editor
Carol Wilson Mansfield, Art Director
Linda Causee, Editor
Meredith Montross, Associate Editor
Christina Wilson, Assistant Editor
Ann Campbell, Illustrations
Graphic Solutions inc-chgo, Book Design

Shown on front cover: Floral Quartet, Windblown Tulips,
Tulips in the Dark, Tulip Garden and It's the Berries.

©1995 by Nancy Brenan Daniel. Published by American School of Needlework®; ASN Publishing, 1455 Linda Vista Drive, San Marcos, CA 92069

ISBN:0-88195-742-9   All rights reserved.   Printed in U.S.A.   4 5 6 7 8 9

About the Designer

Nancy Brenan Daniel, of Tempe, Arizona, has been an art teacher since 1965 and has been teaching quilt making since 1971.

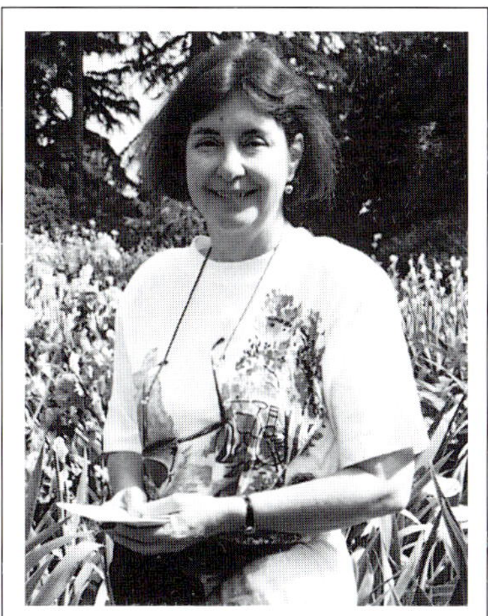

She is the granddaughter of lifelong quilter, Mary Talkington Ritzenthaler of Columbus, Indiana. Her mother, Mary Brenan, finished her first quilt at age 75 and her second quilt at 82.

Nancy earned a bachelor's and master's degree in fine arts, with emphasis in art history. She writes for sewing related publications. Her quilts, garments, and dolls are exhibited in numerous galleries, museums and collections.

Nancy lives in the Arizona desert with her husband Norm, a university professor, and her cats Inky Joseph and Elky Jane. They have three adult children, Karen, David and Stephen. Nancy is an avid gardener.

The American School of Needlework has previously published two rotary technique quilting books by Nancy:

Delectable Mountains: A New View - Book # 4145

Stitch It, Snip It and Flip It - Book #4147

Acknowledgments

My sincerest thanks to Becky Klein for sharing her Tulip Garden quilt, to Stephanie Cornet for machine quilting the Flowering Garden and the Tulip Bed, and to my studio assistants Inky Joseph and Elky Jane. Very special thanks to my husband, friends, quilting students, editors and the many people who contributed their talents during the preparation of this book and who are the source of generous encouragement and advice.

Table of Contents

Introduction

This book is written to fulfill every quilter's desire for floral quilts that are quick and easy and have little appliqué. The easy rotary cut strips and squares for these floral Log Cabin Blocks are accurately cut and machine sewn by any novice. The process can quickly translate a box of cotton fabric scraps into wonderful straight cut and sewn floral patterns.

It's smart to use rotary tools and techniques available to quilters today. The quality of the quilts resulting from the use of the sewing machine and rotary tools are, for the most part, superior in regard to piecing accuracy, design and wearability. As a result, quilters can make truly beautiful and useful quilts faster than at any time in our history.

In this book, the patterns and combinations of techniques are different and varied. Who would imagine that quilt patterns with names like—Primrose Path, Folk Tulip Bouquet, Windblown Tulips and Flowering Garden are created using the beloved Log Cabin and the Stitch It, Snip It and Flip It quick piecing techniques.

As you read through all the instructions and look at the designs, I hope you will see the possibilities for quilt designs beyond those in the photographed quilts. You'll see that I've added a bit of spice to the quick quilt by mixing techniques. Now everyone can make stunning floral patterns—without complicated techniques.

Nancy Brenan Daniel

General Directions

Choosing Fabrics

Generally the best fabrics for rapid piecing techniques are those which do not stretch while being cut and those that do not fray. Choose 100% cottons for their ease in handling. Cotton fabrics hold their shape and are easiest to cut and sew accurately. Cotton blends may be combined with 100% cotton fabrics if they are of equal weight, weave and thickness. Using cotton blends will require extra care in cutting and sewing for accuracy.

Pre-wash all fabric. Some quilt historians feel that pre-washed quilt fabrics devalue the quilt. That may or may not be true. I recommend pre-washing all quilt fabric to test for colorfastness and to make sure the fabric is pre-shrunk. Wash light and dark fabrics separately. Rinse the fabric until the water is clear of excess dyes.

Press the fabric to remove wrinkles. Use a spray sizing to add body to the washed fabrics—especially cotton blends. The sizing is helpful in creating accurate cuts and stabilizing bias edges. When pressing cotton blended fabric, extra care must be taken. Some of these fabrics are very sensitive to the hotter temperatures used with 100% cotton fabrics.

Fabric yardage for all quilts is estimated for 44" wide fabrics.

Color

There are no bad colors. Choose any color harmony you enjoy for your patchwork garden of quilts. Look to nature for your color inspiration if you are unsure. Fields of wildflowers are riots of glorious color harmonies.

The value (measurement of light and dark) of a color is important. Value defines the design and the character of color. The color value of the fabrics used can even change within a quilt. The dramatic Windblown Tulips quilt on the back cover, illustrates the interchange of color value along the diagonal of the quilt—from upper left to lower right.

Choose fabric with good color and textural contrast for the flowers and leaves.

The Flowering Garden Quilt shown on page 24, is another example of using color value to define and control the weight of design and color in quilting. Notice the amount of green fabric around the center of the quilt. The leaves are more effective because of the controlled placement of green color values in alternating lights and darks. Without this control the area with the green piecing would seem, visually, to be too heavy.

Supplies

Sewing Machine: Use a straight stitch for piecing and a zigzag stitch for machine appliqué.

Needles: Use sewing machine needles for cotton fabrics. Change needles often.

Threads: Use good quality cotton or cotton-covered polyester all-purpose threads.

Seam Ripper: Sharp, safety-tipped tool for removing stitches.

Scissors: Sharp fabric scissors for trimming fabric and clipping thread.

Marking Tools: Light and dark, removable fabric markers as well as a #2 pencil.

Rotary Tools: Rotary cutter, cutting mat, and 6" x 24" clear acrylic ruler are a must. Other rulers, 6" x 12", 3" x 12" and 12" x 12" are good to have.

Rotary blades are known to stay sharp longer when only 100% cotton fabrics are cut. Have extra blades on hand. Remove and discard blades safely.

Stylus or Extra Long Needle: For pushing fabric toward the sewing machine needle.

Rotary Cutting Basics

First, straighten the grain of the fabric by pulling at opposite corners. First pull in one direction and then in the opposite direction, **Fig 1**.

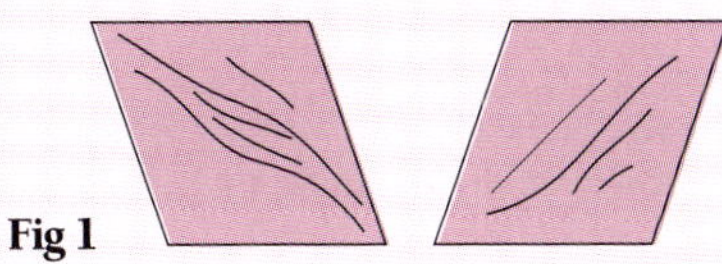

Fig 1

Before you cut your fabric, write down the number of strips, squares and pieces required for your project. Post your note close to the cutting table and refer to it often to keep track of the amount of fabric you've cut. It's easy to cut up fabric that needs to be reserved for another part of the quilt.

Before sewing, check your machine for an accurate 1/4" seam allowance. An accurate 1/4" seam allowance is critical. Sewing an inaccurate seam allowance can mean a near disaster when machine sewing and rapid piecing. For example, a mere 1/16" error repeated over seven seams equals almost a 1/2" mistake in seam allowances (and that's if you figure only one side of the seam!).

Cutting the Fabric

Fold fabric in half, selvage to selvage, **Fig 2**. The folded edge should be smooth and the selvages even. The fabric needs to be flat and smooth for accurate cutting.

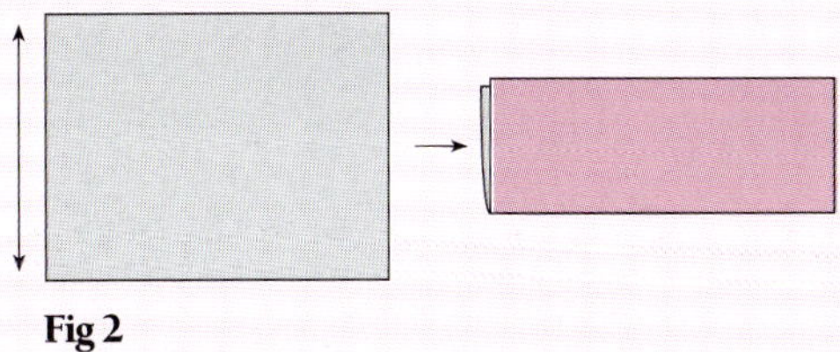

Fig 2

Place the folded fabric along one of the horizontal lines on the cutting mat. (Add accurate horizontal and vertical lines to your mat if it does not have a grid.) The grid lines are important for making straight cuts. The fabric will extend to the right for right-handed people, or extend to the left for left-handed people, **Fig 3**.

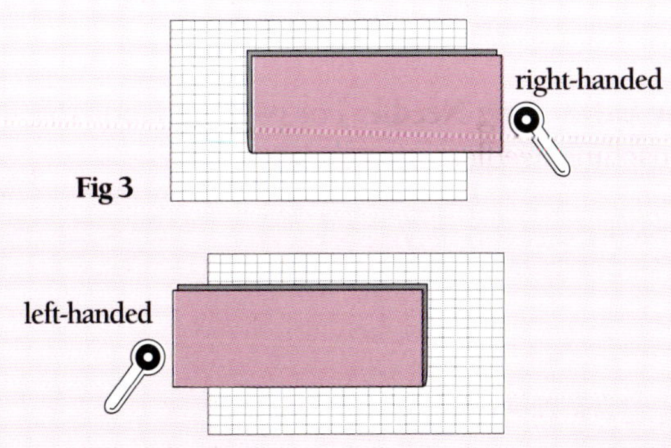

Fig 3

Lay the ruler along one of the vertical lines of the mat, **Fig 4**. The fabric must be absolutely horizontal to the vertical ruler for accurate cutting. Rest the open rotary blade flush against the acrylic ruler; press down firmly. Begin cutting away from you on the mat. Cut through the doubled width of the fabric with one clean movement. After each cut, straighten the fabric to the horizontal line and reposition ruler to a vertical line, making sure you have a 90° angle. Think of the carpenter's tool each time you square up. Leave strips folded until needed. Pin a written identification label to all stacks of cut squares and strips.

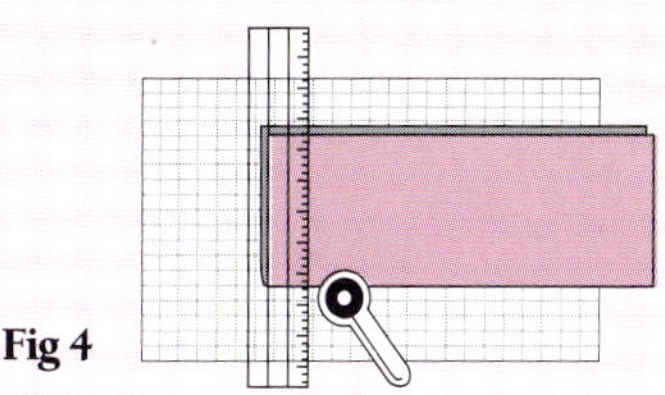

Fig 4

• Rotary cutters will cut up to twelve layers at a time. Experiment to determine the number of layers you are able to cut with accuracy.

• Close the rotary cutting tool after each cut.

• Keep fingers, hands, arms and other body parts away from the cutting edge of the blade. Do not make a hand gesture with the cutter in your hand!

• Place cutting mat on a flat surface.

• Always measure twice and cut once!

Sewing Guidelines, Terms and Tips

• To make longer binding or border strips join two or more cut strips by making a diagonal seam, **Fig 5**. Trim excess fabric 1/4" from seam and press seam open.

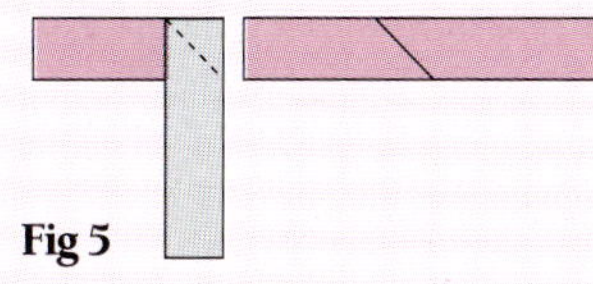

Fig 5

• All seams are sewn with right sides together unless otherwise stated.

• All seams are sewn with a 1/4" seam allowance.

• Press all seams toward the darker fabric whenever practical.

• Press seams to one side, and not open, unless otherwise stated.

continued

Terms

Finger Press: Open a small stitched seam and firmly, without stretching, press flat with the balls of your finger tips.

Skip Block: An unpieced block placed between pieced blocks.

Strip Piecing: Sewing long strips of fabric to each other or to previously sewn units.

Chain Piecing: Sewing a complete group of one type of unit in one continuous, long chain, **Fig 6**.

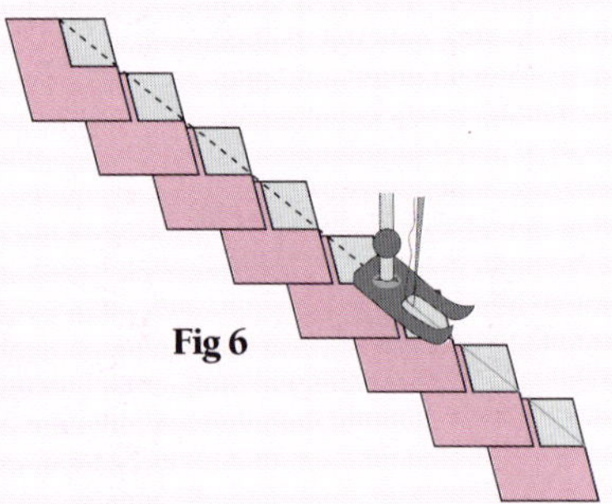

Fig 6

Squaring the Blocks: Measuring, and trimming if necessary, pieced blocks so they will be the same size. Do not trim off your 1/4" seam allowance.

Log Cabin Technique: A particular way of strip piecing together a block in a spiral pattern, **Fig 7**. Blocks should always be pieced in the same direction unless the pattern states otherwise.

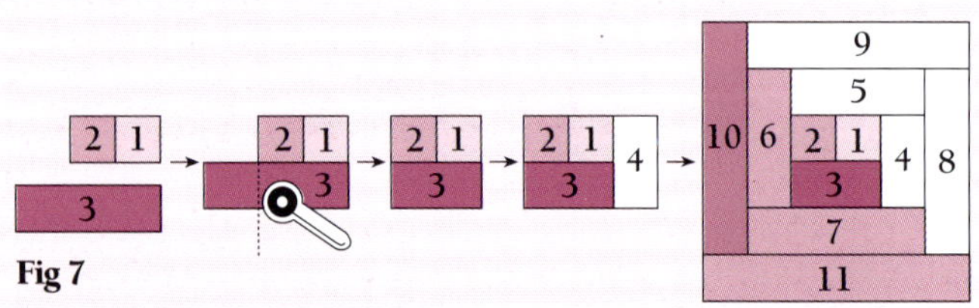

Fig 7

Stitch It, Snip It and Flip It Technique: Stitching a square to another shape, cutting the excess fabric away and flipping it over, **Fig 8**. This piecing short-cut is a very old technique and is even used in hand piecing. I learned it from my grandmother and gave the technique its name in my American School of Needlework® book, Stitch It, Snip It and Flip It .

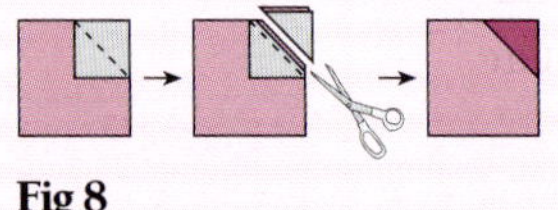

Fig 8

Basic Hand and Machine Appliqué

Easy Hand Technique

1. Trace appliqué design onto the paper side of plastic coated freezer paper. Cut design from paper.

2. Iron paper onto wrong side of appliqué fabric. Cut around shape leaving a 1/8" to 1/4" seam allowance.

3. Fold seam allowance over paper piece; make a crisp edge. When working with a pointed such as a leaf, fold one side over the paper and glue with a glue stick; then fold the other side over and glue in place, **Fig 9**. Do not clip excess at points.

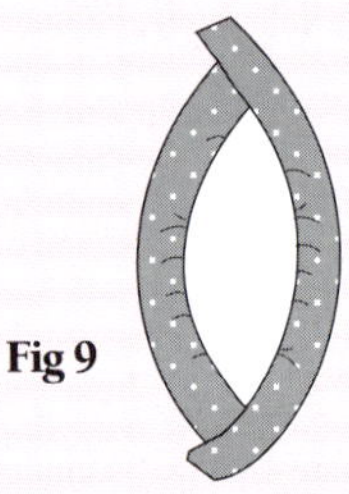

Fig 9

4. Position the appliqué piece and stitch to the background fabric using matching thread and close hidden stitches, **Fig 10**. Tuck in excess fabric at points with needle as you finish the leaf points.

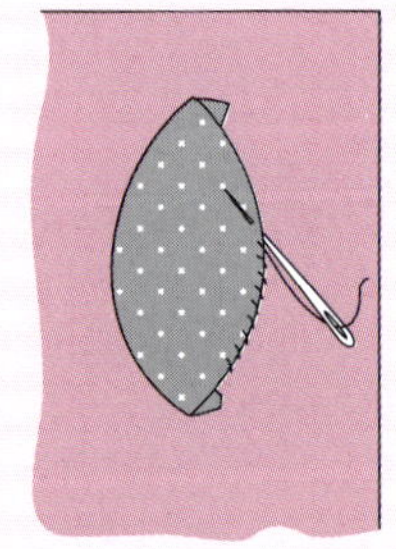

Fig 10

Easy Machine Technique

1. Trace appliqué shapes onto paper backing of lightweight fusible web.

2. Press webbing on wrong side of fabric, following manufacturer's directions, **Fig 11**.

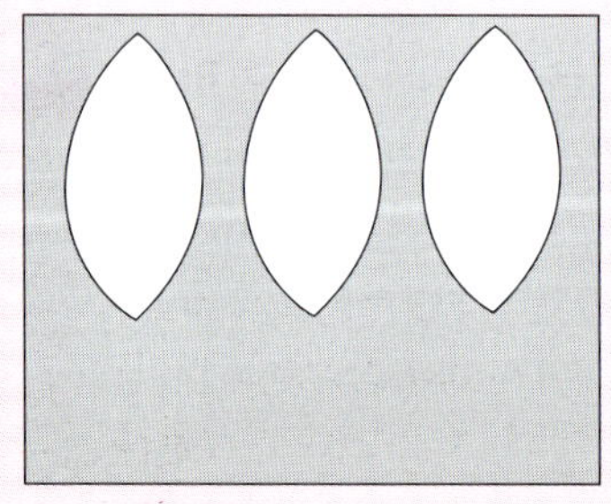

Fig 11

3. Cut shapes from fused fabric; peel off paper backing. Position piece, web side down onto background fabric; fuse with an iron according to the manufacturer's directions.

4. Zigzag over the raw edge with matching thread using a close zigzag pattern, **Fig 12**.

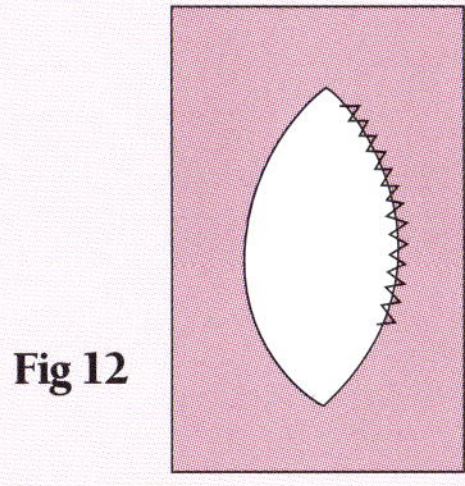

Fig 12

Assembling the Quilt Top

Straight Set Quilt

1. Arrange blocks and other quilt parts according to individual quilt diagram.

2. Sew blocks and other quilt parts together in horizontal rows. Press seams in opposite directions from row to row, **Fig 13**.

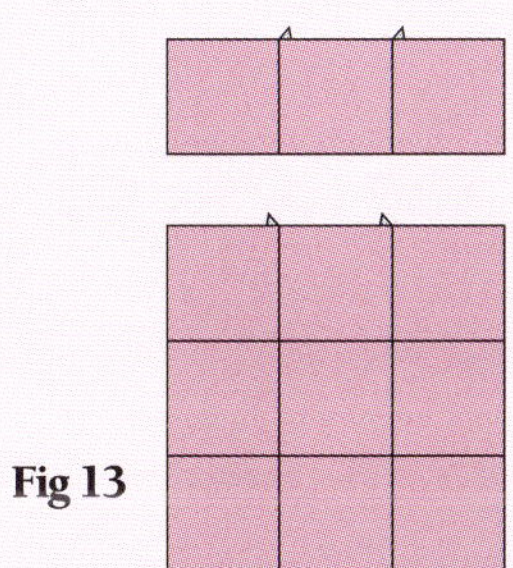

Fig 13

3. Sew the rows together making sure to match the seams between the blocks or added sections whenever possible, **Fig 14**.

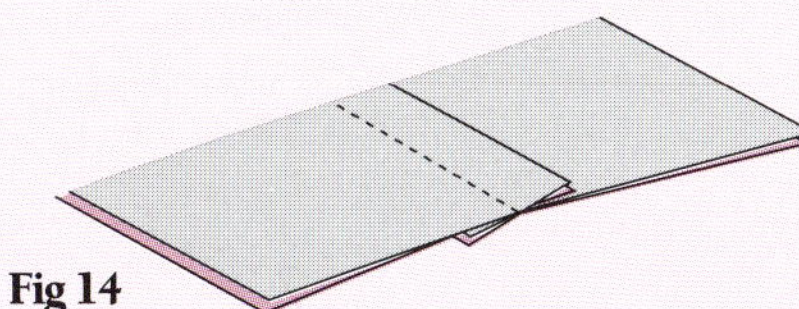

Fig 14

Diagonally Set Quilt

1. Arrange blocks, finishing triangles and corner triangles according to individual quilt diagram.

2. Sew together in diagonal rows. Press joining seams in opposite directions from row to row.

3. Sew rows together. Match appropriate seams between the blocks, **Fig 15**.

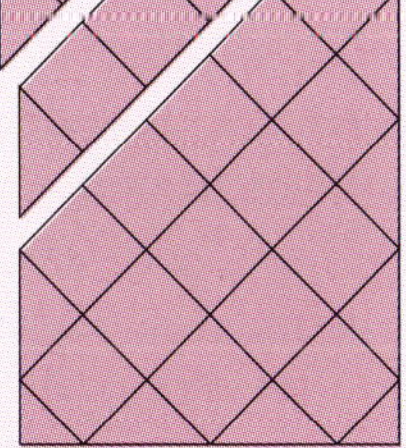

Fig 15

Finishing Instructions

After quilt top has been given a final pressing, prepare the top for borders by making sure all corners and sides are straight and square. The top and bottom of the quilt should be the same measurement and the side measurements should match.

Trim with rotary tools if necessary, making sure to leave a 1/4" seam allowance beyond all pieced points.

Simple Borders

1. Cut border fabric to match top and bottom quilt measurements, **Fig 16**.

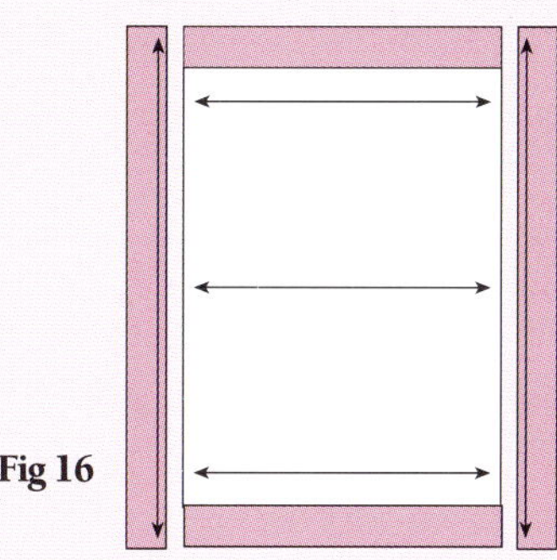

Fig 16

2. Pin borders to top and bottom of quilt at the ends and in the center.

3. Sew borders to quilt top.

4. Re-measure each side of quilt top including borders and cut border strips to this measurement.

5. Pin borders to sides of quilt at ends and in middle.

6. Sew borders to quilt.

7. For additional borders repeat steps 1 to 6.

Borders with Corner Squares

1. Cut border strips to the top and bottom measurement.

2. Sew borders to quilt top. Press toward outside of quilt top.

3. Cut border fabric to the true, original, measurement of the sides of the quilt top (not including top and bottom borders).

4. Cut four squares of fabric using the width of the border fabric measurement. For example, a 3"-wide border strip will need a 3" x 3" square.

continued

5. Stitch squares to ends of side borders before sewing to quilt, **Fig 17**. Finger press seams toward border strip.

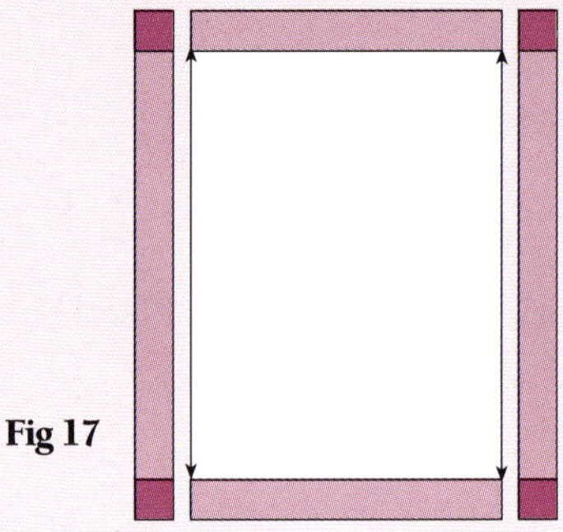

Fig 17

6. Sew borders to sides of quilt matching seams at corner blocks.

Prepare for Quilting or Machine Tacking

Marking the Quilt

Plan quilting designs and method of quilting (by hand or machine) before layering backing, batting and quilt top.

Mark quilting lines on right side of quilt top. Use a removable marking pencil, pen, or other quilt marking tool. Test all marking tools before using on your quilt. Follow all manufacturer's instructions.

Batting and Backing

We have indicated the amount of fabric and batting required for each pattern.

Use an appropriate batting for the end use of the quilt. Read manufacturer's specifications for use. I prefer bonded polyester batting for tied, machine tacked quilts, and some hand quilting.

Needle-punched or bonded cotton battings are good for machine quilting and some are good for hand quilting.

Since several of the quilts in the book are wider than most fabric widths, you will have to sew lengths of fabric together to make the backing. Cut off selvages and seam pieces together carefully. Press seams open.

Layering the Quilt

Cut batting and backing larger than the quilt top—about 2" wider than the top on all sides. Place backing, wrong side up, on a flat surface. Place batting on top of this, matching outer edges. It is a good idea to remove batting from its packaging a day in advance and open it out full size. This will help the batting to lie flat and relax.

Center quilt top with right side up on top of batting.

Basting the Layers

The layers of the quilt are basted either with thread or with safety pins before quilting.

For **thread basting**, pin backing, batting and quilt top together. Baste with long stitches, starting at center of quilt and working toward outside of quilt. Create a number of long diagonal lines of stitching.

For pin basting, pin the backing, batting and quilt top together at six-inch intervals using size 0 or 1 safety pins. Start in the middle and work toward outside. Avoid placing pins in prospective quilting lines.

Do not trim excess backing or batting after basting.

Quilting and Machine Tacking

Quilting can be done by hand, machine, tying or tacking. Whatever method you choose, start quilting in the center and work toward the outside edges.

Hand Quilting

To quilt by hand, place basted quilt in a quilting hoop or frame. Using a small needle (betweens #7 to #12) and quilting thread, make small, even running-like stitches along quilting lines. Hand quilting for pieced projects often follows 1/4" outside seam. Hand quilting for appliqué projects often follows 1/16" to 1/8" outside design.

Machine Quilting with Feed Dogs Up

The feed dogs control the forward and backward motion of the quilt through the sewing machine.

To quilt by machine, use a fine transparent nylon thread or 100% cotton machine thread for the top. Use cotton or cotton covered polyester in the bobbin. Never use nylon thread in your bobbin. An even-feed foot is a good investment if you are going to machine quilt since it feeds the top and bottom layers through the machine evenly and helps prevent puckers.

In order to fit a large quilt under the arm of the sewing machine, it will be necessary to fold the quilt so it is more manageable. If you are quilting in horizontal or vertical lines, the first row of quilting will be done in the center. Starting at the sides, roll the quilt to within 4" to 5" of center seam; then roll quilt up from the bottom to within a few inches of where you will begin sewing. If you are quilting diagonally, your first row of quilting will go from one corner to the opposite corner. Roll the quilt to within 4" to 5" of that first diagonal quilting line. Then roll quilt up from the bottom corner to within a few inches of where you will be sewing.

With rolled quilt in your lap, place quilt so that you are in the right position to begin. Make sure that you have a table on the other side of the machine to catch the completed work, otherwise the weight of the quilt can cause a problem. Whenever possible work from the center out, re-rolling the quilt as you work.

A short table placed to your left as you machine quilt will help support the weight of the quilt as the quilt moves toward you.

Machine Quilting with Feed Dogs Down

This method is often called hand-guided machine quilting. With this technique you will need a sewing machine darning foot. Place the darning foot on your sewing machine. Properly placed, the foot will not touch the machine foot plate when it is in the down position. Thread the sewing machine for machine quilting. Hand guide basted quilt under darning foot, following the same technique used in dogs up machine quilting. The only difference is that you control the forward movement of fabric along the quilting pattern. Practice.

Machine Tacking the Quilt

A zigzag sewing machine is needed. Set the feed dogs down. Set the width of zigzag to what you want showing as the tacks. Using the same placement techniques as for all quilting, start in the middle of the quilt.

Drop the foot where you want a machine tack. Zigzag, in place until the needle has passed over the same place eight or ten times. Lift the needle and move the quilt to the new spot for tacking. Tack the quilt according to the design. Machine tack at a minimum of 6" intervals. Threads can be cut after all tacking is done. The It's the Berries quilt, page 42, was machine tacked over a very thick polyester batting.

Binding

Place quilt on flat surface and trim backing and batting to the quilt top edge. Measure around the quilt. Cut and join binding strips to that length. Binding width can be 2" to 2 1/2" depending on personal choice.

Next, press the strip in half with wrong side together along the length.

Open the fold and make a long diagonal cut across the bias, **Fig 18**.

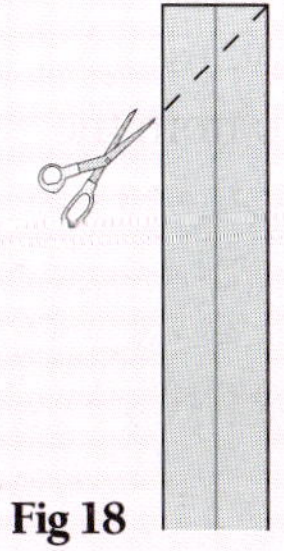

Fig 18

Fold down a 1/4" seam along the bias edge. Refold strip lengthwise, **Fig 19** and apply the binding along the edge of the back of the quilted top, **Fig 20**.

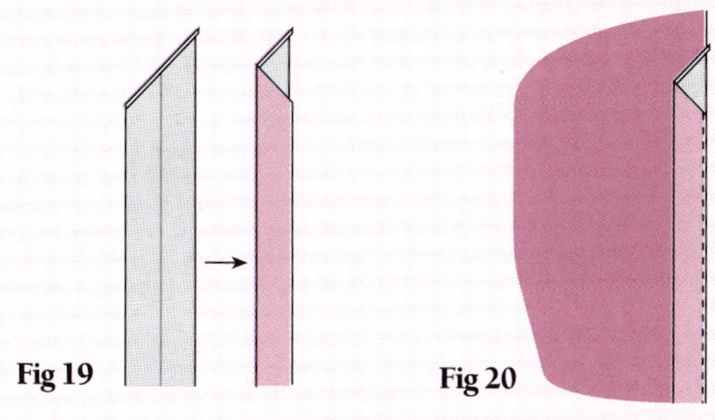

Fig 19

Fig 20

Stitch binding to within a 1/4" seam allowance of the edge of the side.

At the corners, fold the binding at a complete right angle to the stitching. Drop the needle. Pivot around the corner around the dropped needle. Continue stitching around the quilt and completing the corners, **Fig 21**.

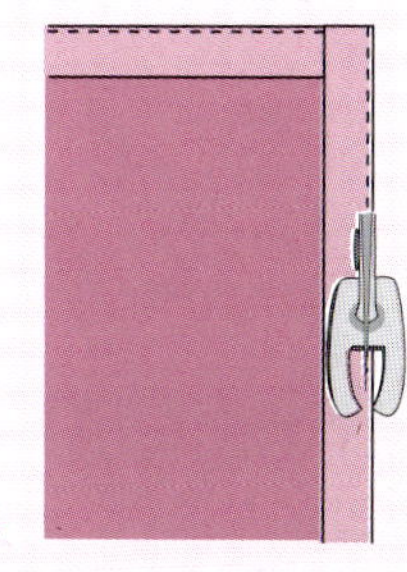

Fig 21

This right angle corner tuck will create a full mitered corner when turned to the right side and stitched down.

To finish the end of the binding, tuck the raw end into the bias cut at the beginning of the binding and finish sewing, **Fig 22**.

Turn binding to the right side of the quilt and stitch down with a hidden slip stitch by hand or a machine hemming stitch. Close the mitered corner tuck with a few additional hand stitches.

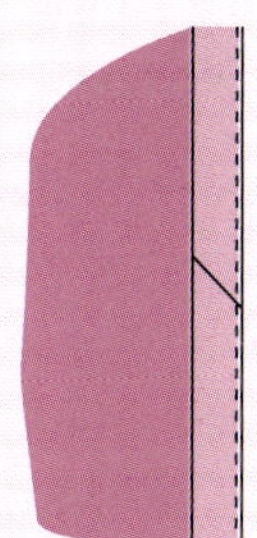

Fig 22

Tulip Garden

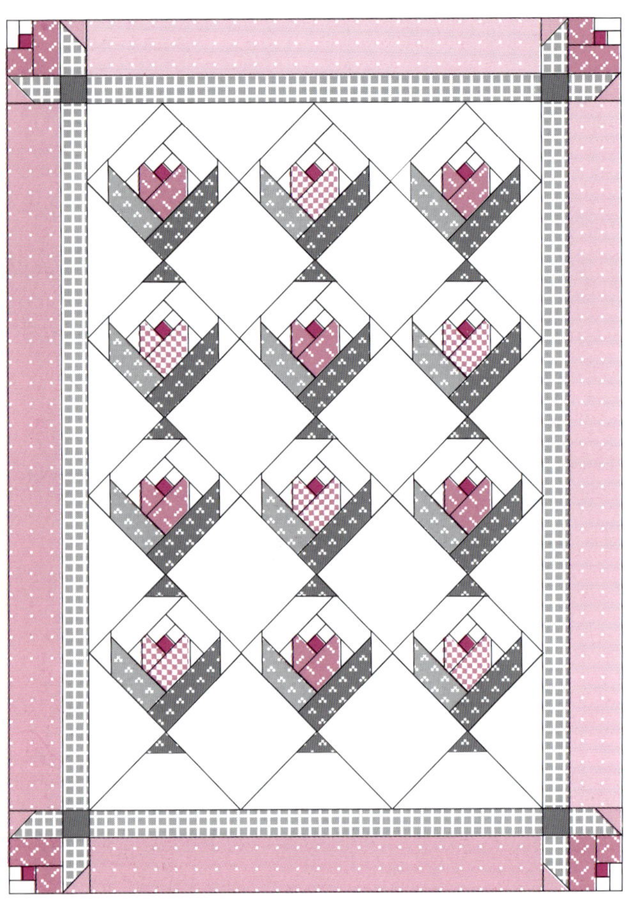

Shown in full color on page 24.

COLOR KEY

- Pink Plaid
- Pink Print
- Dark Rose
- Med Green
- Dk Med Green
- White
- Green Check
- Pink Floral
- Dark Green

APPROXIMATE SIZE: 46" x 63"

FINISHED BLOCK SIZE: 8" x 8"

The crisp design and colors are like a breath of fresh spring air. Sixteen pieced blocks and eight plain skip blocks create this perky pattern. This sample was made by my friend Becky for her new grandchild!

Fabric Requirements:

1/8 yd pink plaid for six tulips
1/4 yd pink print for ten tulips
1/8 yd dk rose for centers
1/3 yd med green for leaves
1/3 yd dk med green for leaves
2 yds white solid for background
1/2 yd green check for first border
3/4 yd pink floral for second border
1/2 yd dk green for corners and binding
2 1/2 yds 44"-wide fabric for backing
twin size batting

Cutting Requirements:

Note: *Cut all strips along the crosswise grain.*
one 2 1/2"-wide strip, pink plaid (tulips)
two 2 1/2"-wide strips, pink print (tulips)
one 1 1/2"-wide strip, dk rose (centers)
five 2 1/2"-wide strips, med green (leaves)
five 2 1/2"-wide strips, dk green (leaves)
twelve 2 1/2" x 2 1/2" squares, med dk green (stems)
24 - 1 1/2" x 1 1/2" squares, white
two 1 1/2"-wide strip, white
seven 2 1/2"-wide strips, white
24 - 2 1/2" x 2 1/2" squares, white
eight 8 1/2" x 8 1/2" squares, white (skip blocks)

four 13" x 13" squares, white (cut diagonally into
   quarters for finishing triangles, **Fig 1**)
one 7" x 7" square, white (cut in half diagonally for
   top corners, **Fig 2**)

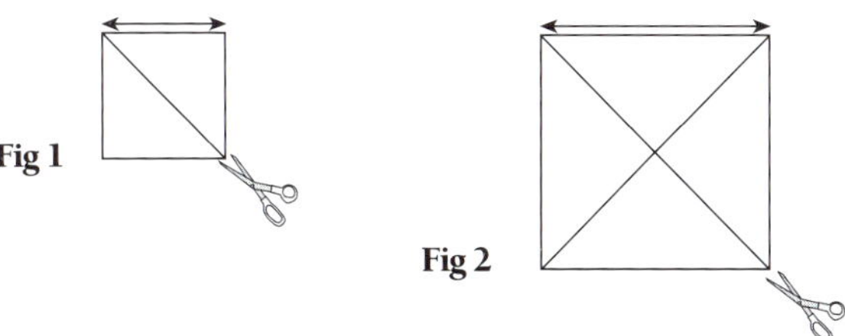

Fig 1

Fig 2

five 2 1/2"-wide strips, green check (first border)
eight 2 1/2" x 4 1/2" rectangles, green check (border tulips)
five 4 1/2"-wide strips, pink floral (second border)
eight 2 1/2" x 2 1/2" squares, pink floral (border tulips)
four 2 1/2" x 2 1/2" squares, dk green (first border squares)
six 2"-wide strips, dk green (binding)

Instructions:

Making the Tulips

1. Stitch the 1 1/2" strips of dark rose center fabric and
background fabric together, **Fig 3**; press seam to dark side.

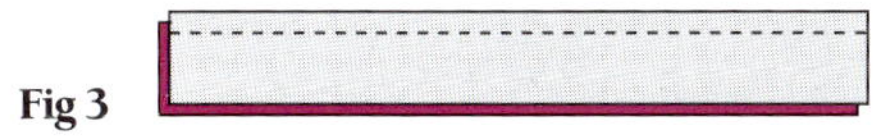

Fig 3

2. Cut into sixteen 1 1/2"-wide units, **Fig 4**; finger press
open.

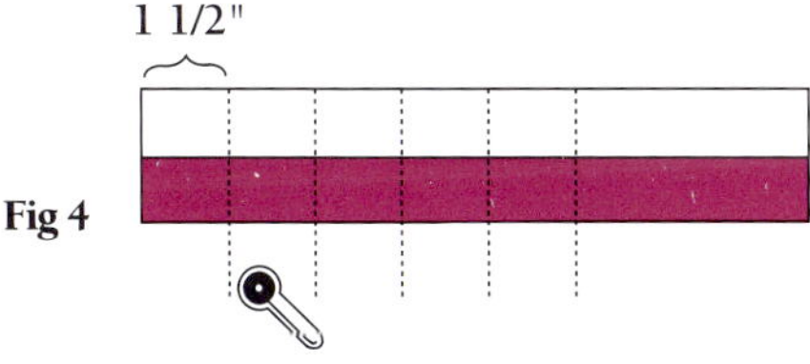

1 1/2"

Fig 4

3. Strip piece these units to 1 1/2"-wide white strip, **Fig 5**;
finger press open.

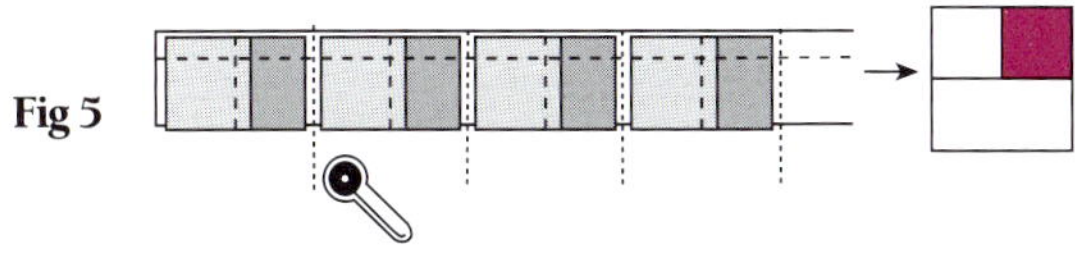

Fig 5

4. Sew ten centers to 2 1/2"-wide pink print strip; sew six
centers to 2 1/2"-wide pink plaid strip. Cut apart and finger
press open, **Fig 6**.

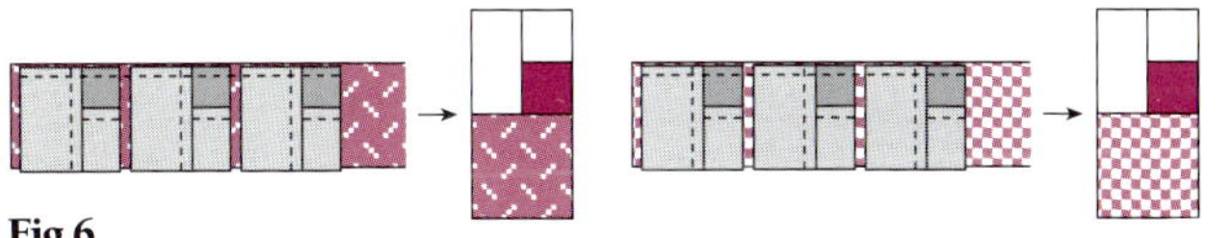

Fig 6

5. Strip piece these units to the matching flower fabric; cut
apart and press open, **Fig 7**. Set aside four tulips from pink
print for border.

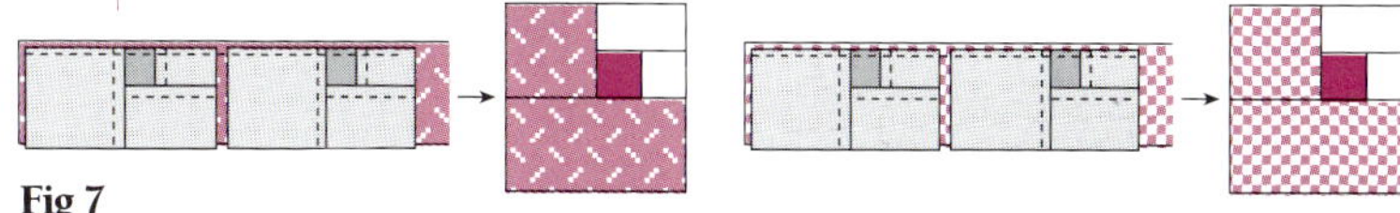

Fig 7

6. Using the Stitch It, Snip It and Flip It Technique, page 8,
stitch the 1 1/2" x 1 1/2" white squares onto corners of six
pink print tulips; trim 1/4" from seam, flip and press, **Fig 8**.

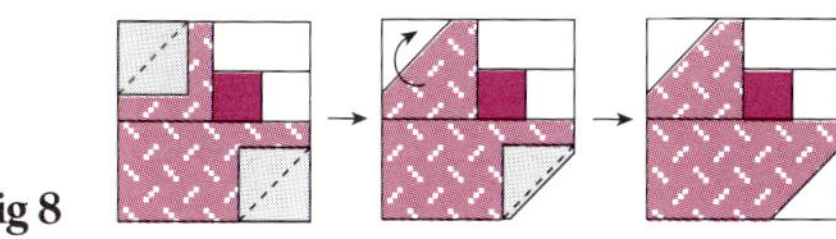

Fig 8

7. Strip piece tulips to 2 1/2"-wide white strip; cut apart and
press. Repeat on second side of tulip, **Fig 9**.

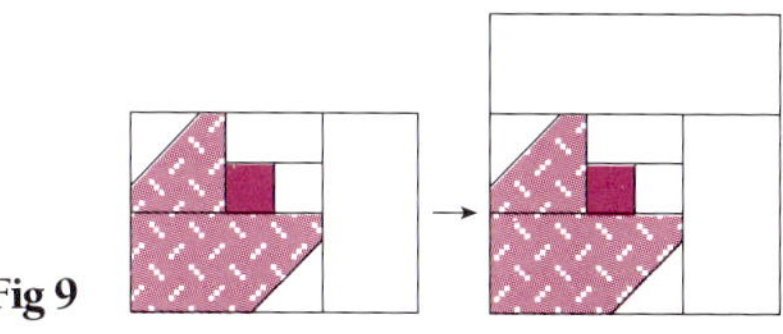

Fig 9

8. Strip piece tulip units to
2 1/2"-wide med green strips; cut
apart and press, **Fig 10**.

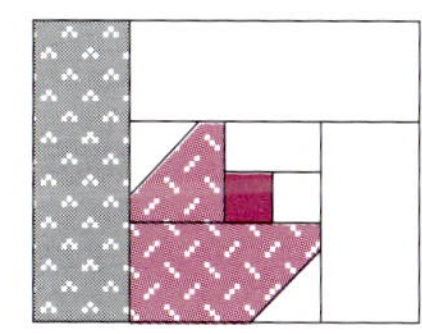

Fig 10

9. Strip piece tulip unit to
2 1/2" wide dk med green strips;
cut apart and press, **Fig 11**.

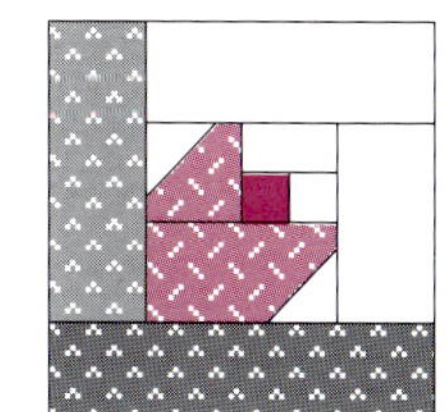

Fig 11

10. Using the Stitch It, Snip It and Flip It technique, page 8,
sew the 2 1/2" x 2 1/2" white squares to ends of leaves; snip
1/4" from seam, flip and press, **Fig 12**.

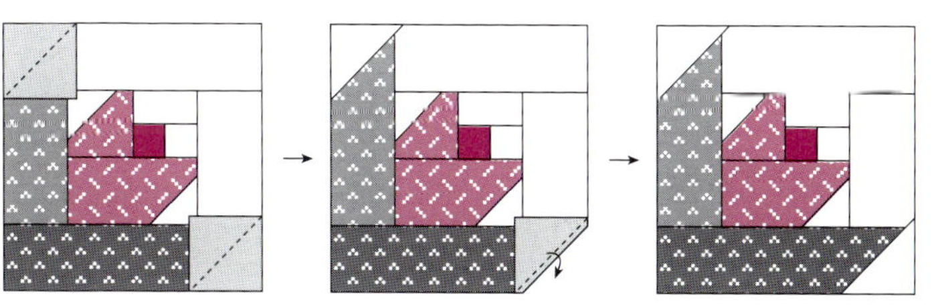

Fig 12

continued

13

11. Repeat steps 6 to 10 for six pink plaid Tulip Blocks, **Fig 13**.

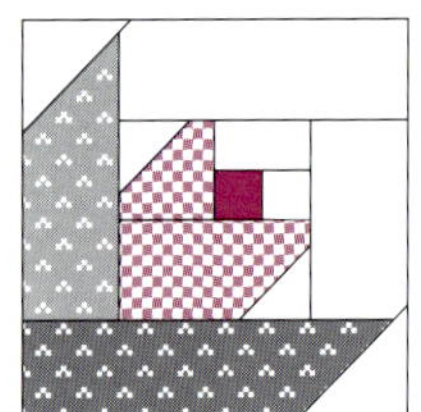

Fig 13

12. Using the same technique, sew a 2 1/2" x 2 1/2" dk med green square to top of five pink plaid tulips and four pink print tulips, **Fig 14**. Repeat for three 13" finishing triangles, **Fig 15**.

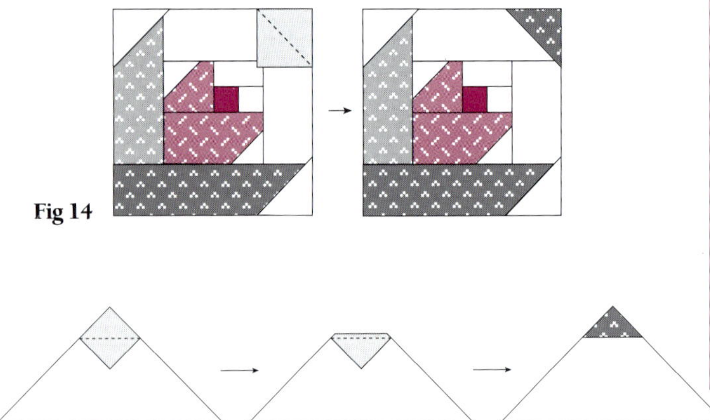

Fig 14

Fig 15

Assembling the Quilt

1. Referring to quilt layout, page 12, place Tulip Blocks, skip blocks, finishing triangles and corner triangles in diagonal rows. Sew together in rows, then sew rows together.

2. For the border tulips, use the four Tulip Blocks set aside in step 5 of Instructions. Stitch one 2 1/2" x 4 1/2" green check rectangle to each tulip block; press toward the outside of the block, **Fig 16**.

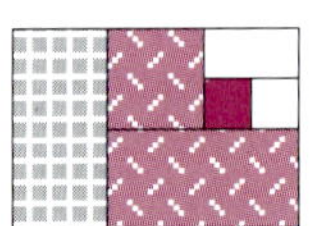

Fig 16

3. Stitch a 2 1/2" x 2 1/2" dk green corner square to end of remaining green check rectangles; stitch to tulip units, **Fig 17**.

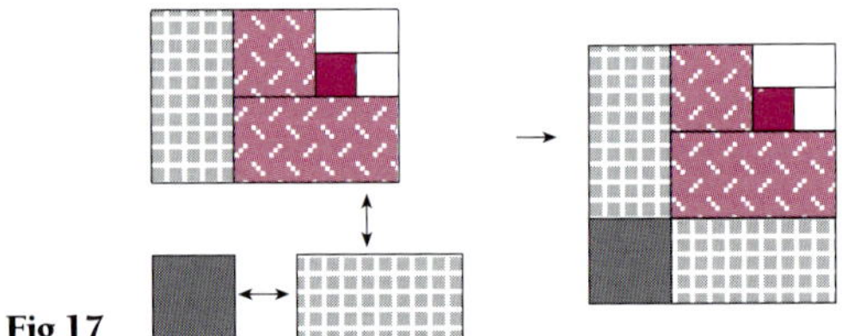

Fig 17

4. Using the Stitch It, Snip It and Flip It technique, page 8, sew 2 1/2" x 2 1/2" pink floral squares to ends of leaves; snip, flip and press, **Fig 18**.

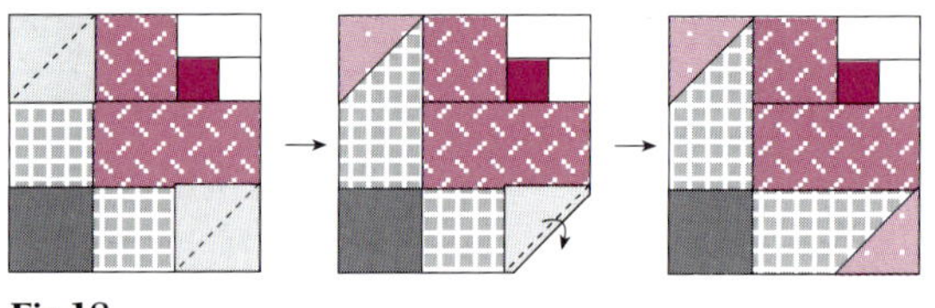

Fig 18

*Note: Refer to **Fig 19** for steps 5 to 9.*

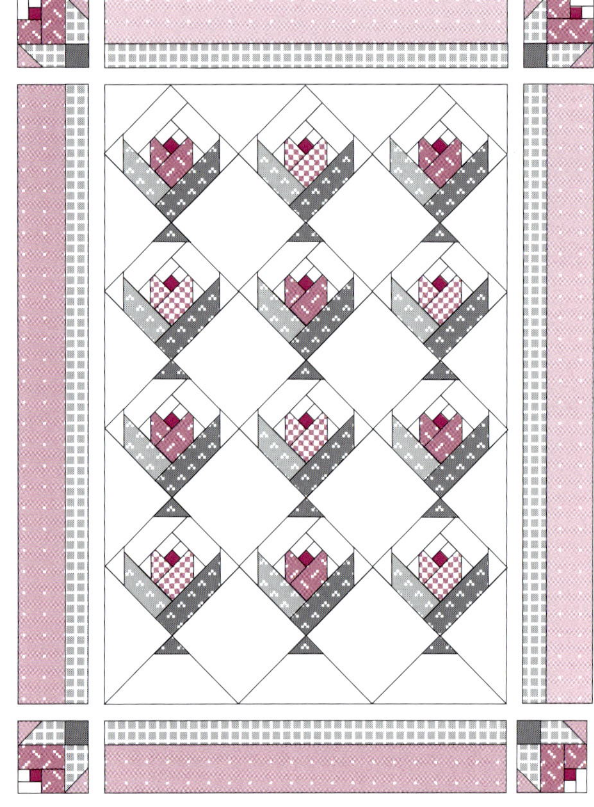

Fig 19

5. Measure width of quilt. Cut two each of first (green check) and second (pink floral) border strips to this size. Sew the strips together then sew to top and bottom of quilt; press toward outside of quilt.

6. Measure length of quilt. Cut (and piece if necessary) two each of first (green check) and second border (pink floral) pieces to this size. Sew borders together but not to quilt; press toward outside pink floral fabric.

7. Sew a Tulip Block to each end of each set of side border strips. Press seams toward borders and not the pieced blocks.

8. Sew these borders to sides of quilt. Press seams toward outside of quilt.

9. Refer to General Directions, pages 9 to 11, to finish your quilt.

Primrose Path

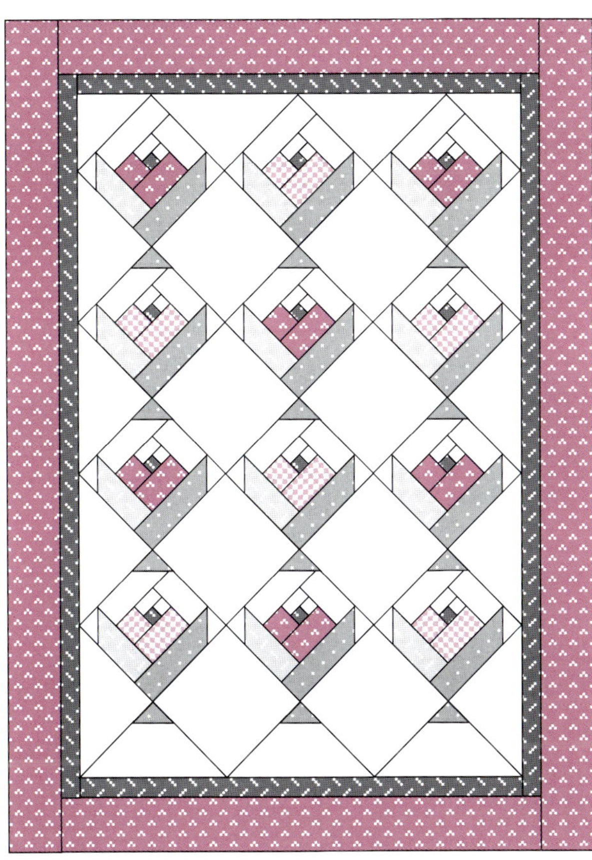

Shown in full color on page 23.

COLOR KEY

	Gold Print
	Yellow Floral
	Black/White Check
	Lt Green
	Med Green
	White

APPROXIMATE SIZE: 45" x 61"

FINISHED BLOCK SIZE: 8" x 8"

This summer bouquet design is reminiscent of the colors and Art Deco quilt styles popular in the 1920s and 1930s. Twelve easy to piece blocks and eight plain skip blocks create this timeless pattern. Make it today...enjoy it tomorrow.

Fabric Requirements:

1/8 yd gold print for six tulips
1/8 yd yellow floral for six tulips
1/8 yd black/white check for centers
1/3 yd lt green for leaves
1/3 yd med green for leaves
2 yds white for background
1/3 yd black/white check for first border
1 1/4 yds yellow floral for second border and binding
2 1/2 yds 44"-wide fabric for backing
twin size batting

Cutting Requirements:

Note: Cut all strips along the crosswise grain.
one 2 1/2"- wide strip, gold print (tulips)
one 2 1/2"-wide strip, yellow floral (tulips)
one 1 1/2"-wide strip, black/white check (centers)
two 2 1/2"-wide strips, lt green (leaves)
three 2 1/2"-wide strips, med green (leaves)
twelve squares 2 1/2" x 2 1/2", med green
two 1 1/2"-wide strips, white background
seven 2 1/2"-wide strips, white background
24 - 2 1/2" x 2 1/2" squares, white
five 2"-wide strips, black/white check (first border)
six 4 3/4"-wide strips, yellow floral (second border)
six 2"-wide strips, yellow floral (binding)
four 13" x 13" squares, white (cut diagonally into quarters for finishing triangles, **Fig 1**)
one 7" x 7" square, white (cut in half diagonally for top corners, **Fig 2**)
eight 8 1/2" x 8 1/2" squares, white (skip blocks)

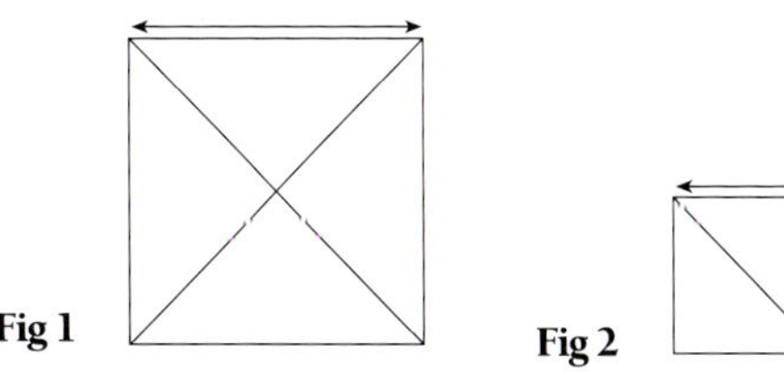

continued

Instructions:

Making the Tulips

1. Stitch 1 1/2" strips of black/white check fabric and white background fabric together, **Fig 3**; press seam to dark side.

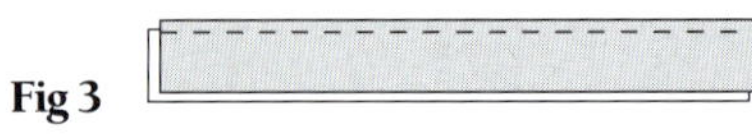

Fig 3

2. Cut into twelve 1 1/2"-wide units, **Fig 4**; finger press open.

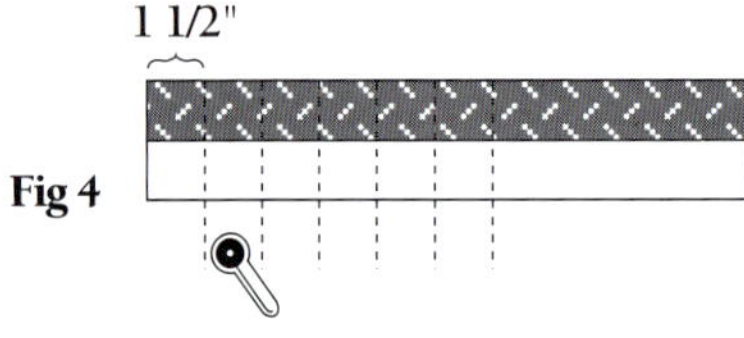

Fig 4

3. Strip piece these units to the 1 1/2"-wide white strip, **Fig 5**; finger press open.

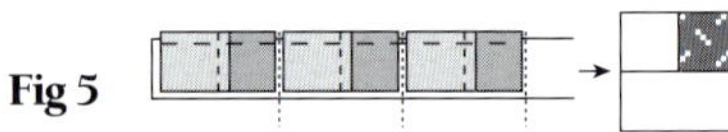

Fig 5

4. Sew six centers to 2 1/2"-wide yellow floral print strip; cut apart and finger press open, **Fig 6**.

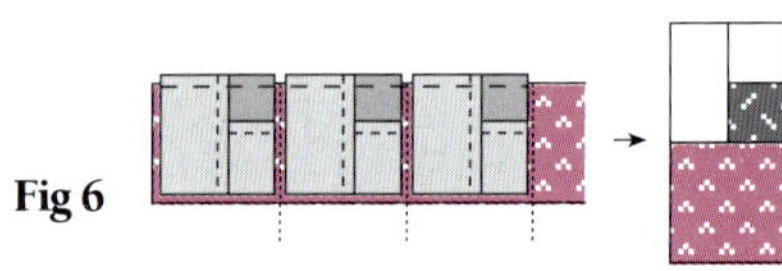

Fig 6

5. Strip piece these units to the matching flower fabric (gold or yellow print); cut apart and press open, **Fig 7**.

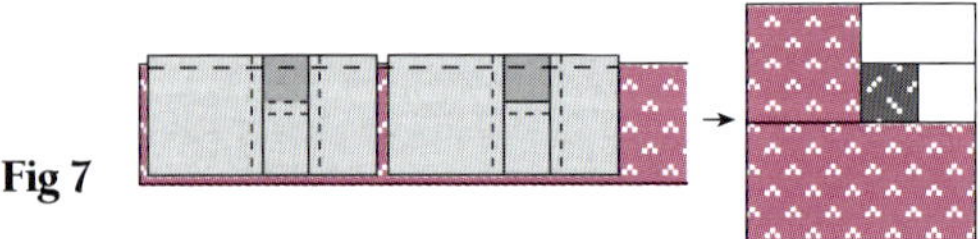

Fig 7

6. Strip piece background strips onto side and then top of tulips, **Fig 8**; press.

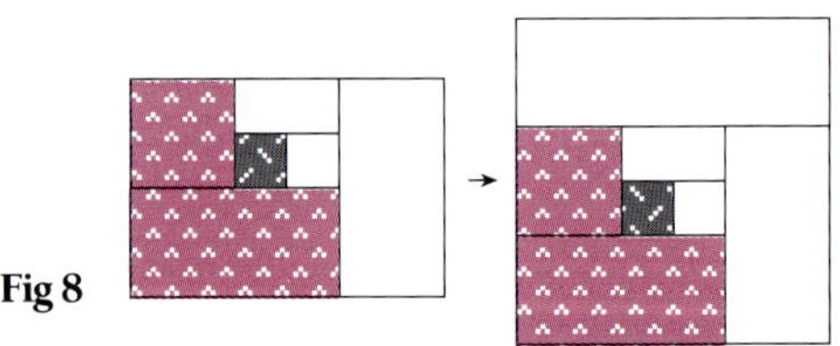

Fig 8

7. Strip piece lt green strips onto tulip units. Press toward the outside of the block after each addition, **Fig 9**. Repeat for med green strips, **Fig 10**.

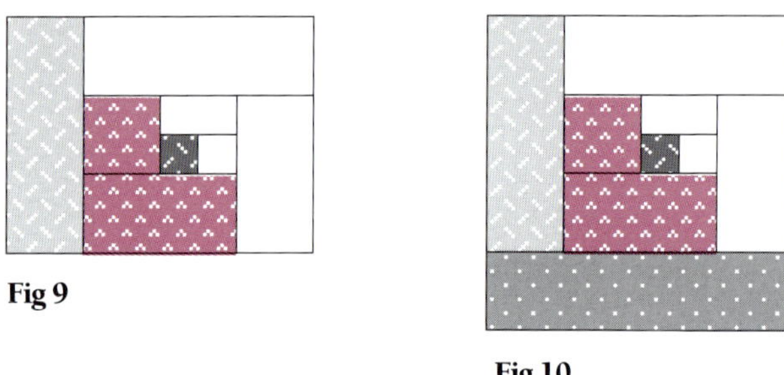

Fig 9

Fig 10

8. Using the Stitch It, Snip It and Flip It technique, page 8, sew the 2 1/2" x 2 1/2" white squares to the ends of the leaves; snip 1/4" from seam, flip and press, **Fig 11**.

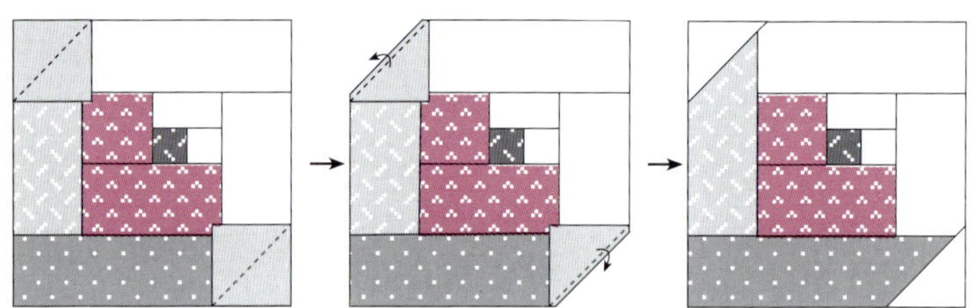

Fig 11

9. Using the same technique, sew a med green 2 1/2" x 2 1/2" square to top of four yellow floral Tulip Blocks, **Fig 12**, and three of the finishing triangles, **Fig 13**.

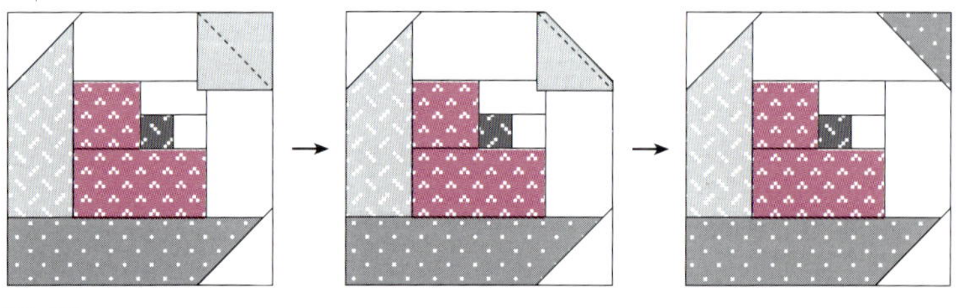

Fig 12

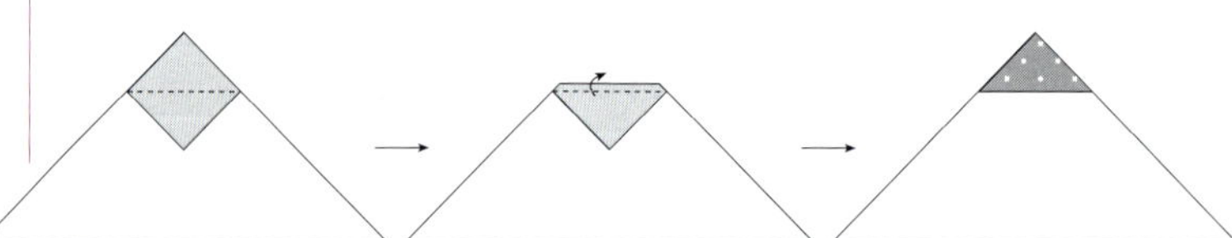

Fig 13

10. Repeat steps 4 to 9 replacing yellow floral strip with 2 1/2"-wide gold print strip, **Fig 14**. *Note: Only five of the six gold print Tulip Blocks have a med green 2 1/2" square added to the top.*

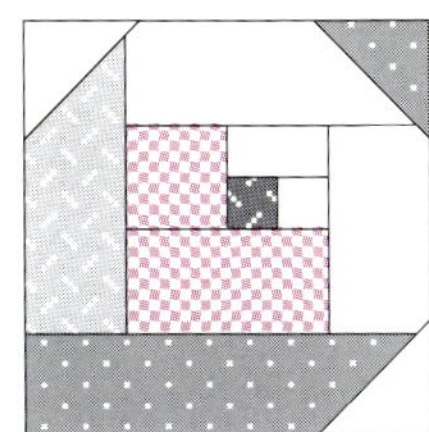

Fig 14

Assembling the Quilt

1. Place Tulip Blocks, skip blocks, finishing triangles and corner triangles in diagonal rows. Sew together in rows, then sew rows together, **Fig 15**.

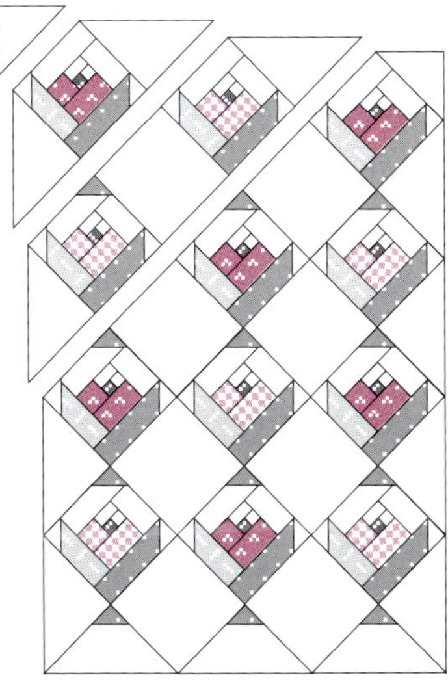

Fig 15

2. Sew first and second borders to quilt referring to Simple Borders, page 9.

3. Refer to General Directions, pages 9 to 11, to finish quilt. The Tulip Quilting Pattern was quilted in the white skip blocks.

Tulip Quilting Pattern

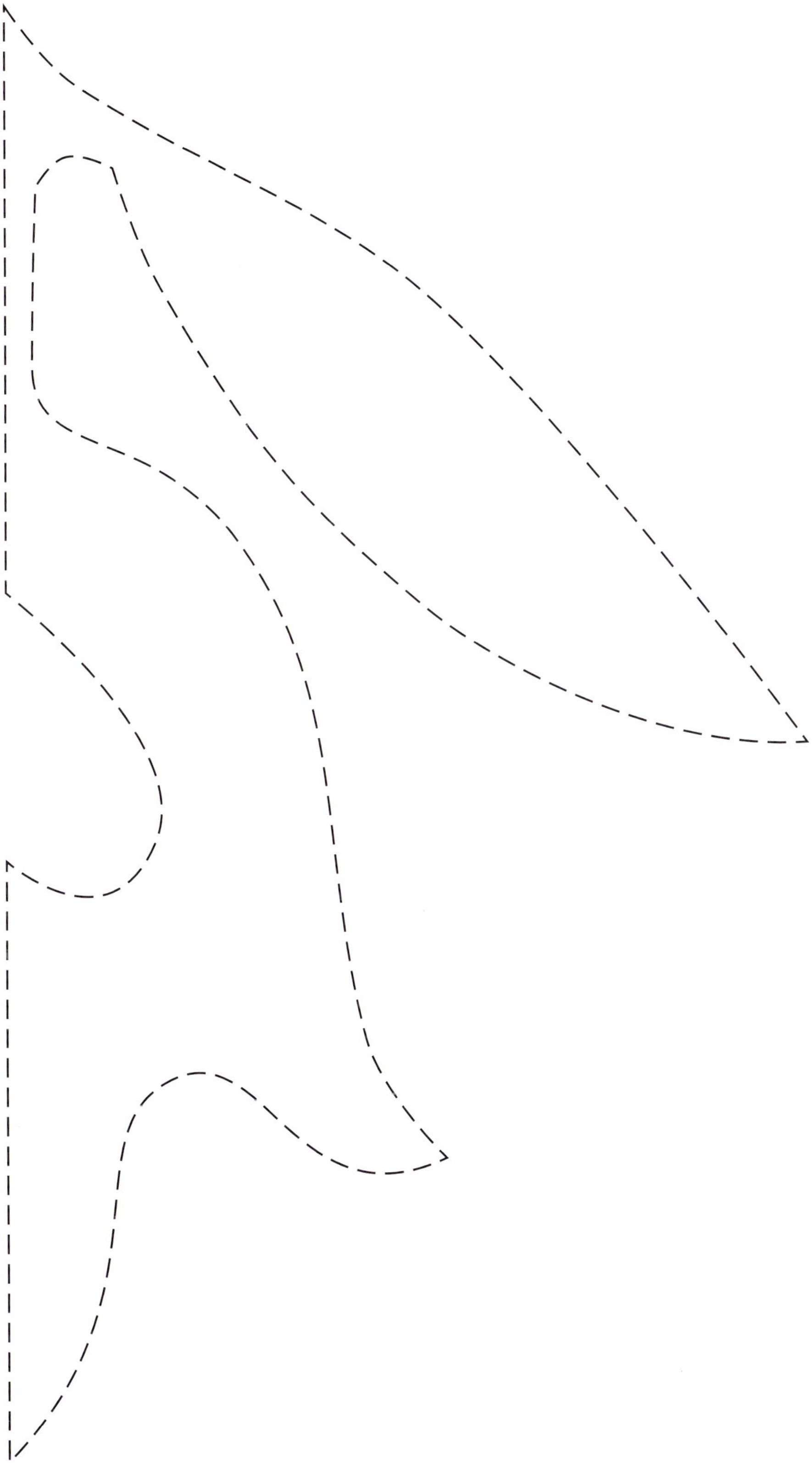

Tulip Bed

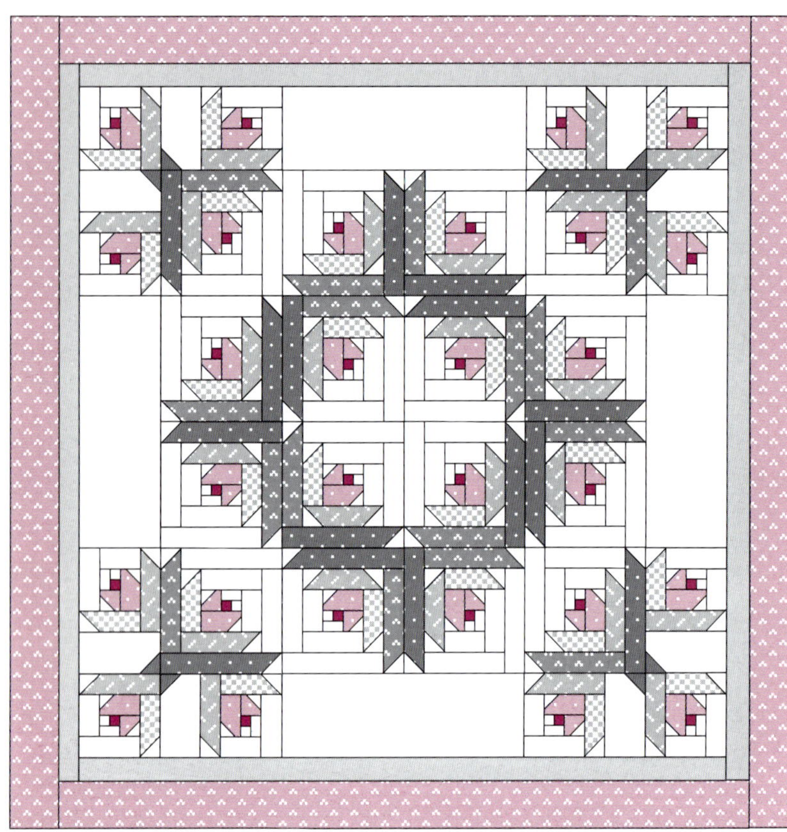

Shown in full color on page 22.

COLOR KEY

- Blue Floral
- Yellow Print
- Green Print 1
- Green Print 2
- Green Print 3
- Green Print 4
- White Floral Print
- Green Plaid
- Dk Floral

APPROXIMATE SIZE: 90" x 90" (to fit full-size bed)

FINISHED BLOCK SIZES: 10" x 10" & 15" x 15"

Fabric Requirements:

1/2 yd blue floral print for tulips
1/8 yd yellow print for centers
2 1/4 yds total of at least four different med
  and dk green prints for leaves
5 1/2 yds white floral print for background
2/3 yd green plaid for first border
1 1/4 yds dk floral for second border
1/2 yd dk floral for binding
3 yds 108"-wide backing fabric
queen/king batting

Cutting Requirements:

five 3"-wide strips, blue floral print (tulips)
two 1 3/4"-wide strips, yellow print (centers)
twenty 3"-wide strips of various green fabrics
  (five strips each of four different prints for leaves)
four 1 3/4"-wide strips, white floral print
  (background)
26 - 3"-wide strips, white floral print (background)
56 - 2" x 2" squares, white floral print (background)
100 - 3" x 3" squares, white floral print (background)
four 10 1/2" x 30 1/2" rectangles, white floral print
  (pieced border)
eight 5 1/2" x 10 1/2" rectangles, white floral print
  (pieced border)
eight 3" x 3" squares, green print (pieced border)
nine 2 1/2"-wide strips, green plaid (first border)
nine 4"-wide strips, dk floral (second border)
nine 2"-wide strips, dk floral (binding)

Instructions:

Making Tulip Block A

1. Strip piece a 1 3/4"-wide yellow print strip and 1 3/4"-wide white floral print strip; press open toward yellow print fabric. Cut strips into 1 3/4"-wide units, **Fig 1**. Make 28.

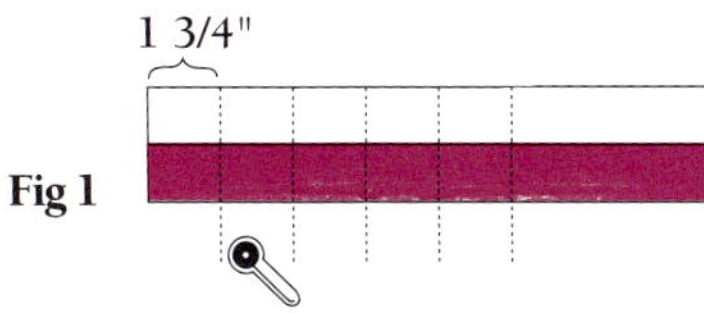

2. Strip piece units to remaining 1 3/4"-wide white floral background strips, **Fig 2**; cut apart and finger press open, **Fig 3**.

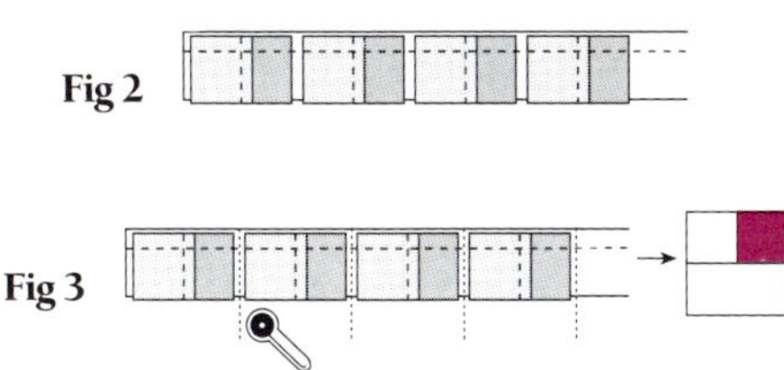

3. Strip piece units to 3"-wide blue floral strips; cut apart and press open, **Fig 4**.

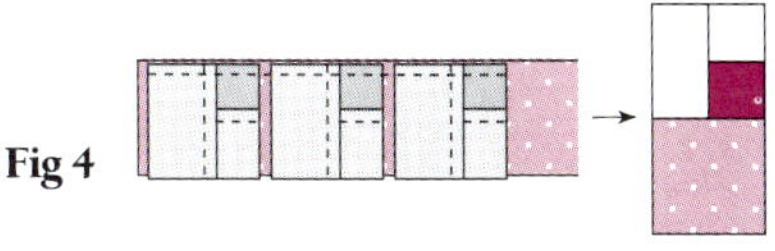

4. Strip piece these units to the remaining 3"-wide blue print strips; cut apart and press, **Fig 5**.

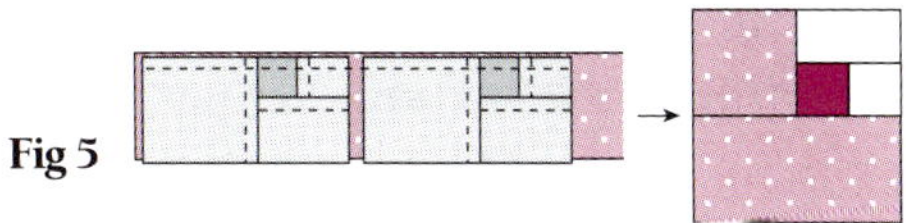

5. Using the Stitch It, Snip It and Flip It technique, page 8, sew 2" white floral square to both sides of tulip, **Fig 6**.

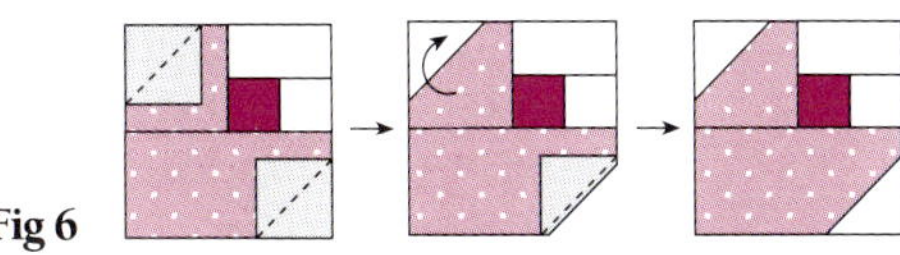

6. Strip piece the 3"-wide white floral background strip to two top sides of unit. Cut apart and press open, **Fig 7**.

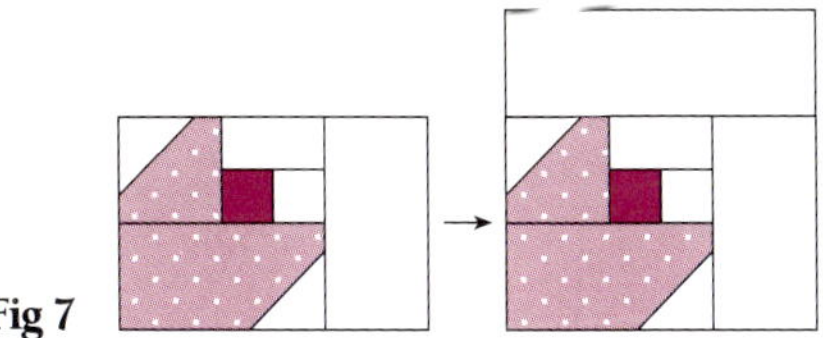

7. Sew two different green print strips to two lower sides of tulip. Cut apart and press, **Fig 8**.

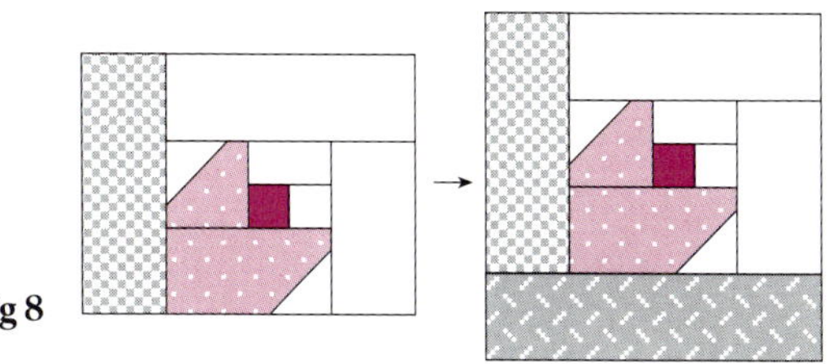

8. Using the Stitch It, Snip It and Flip It technique, sew the 3" white floral squares to tips of both leaves for Tulip Block A; press, **Fig 9**. Set aside twelve Tulip Block As for pieced border.

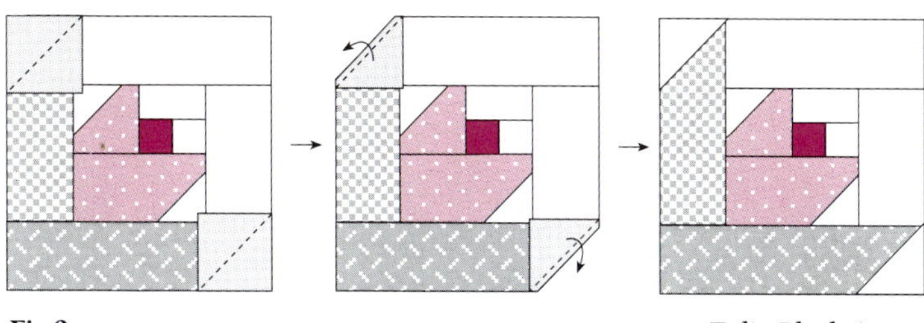

Fig 9   Tulip Block A

Making Tulip Block B

1. Sew one 3" white floral square to bottom of twelve of remaining sixteen Tulip A Blocks, **Fig 10**.

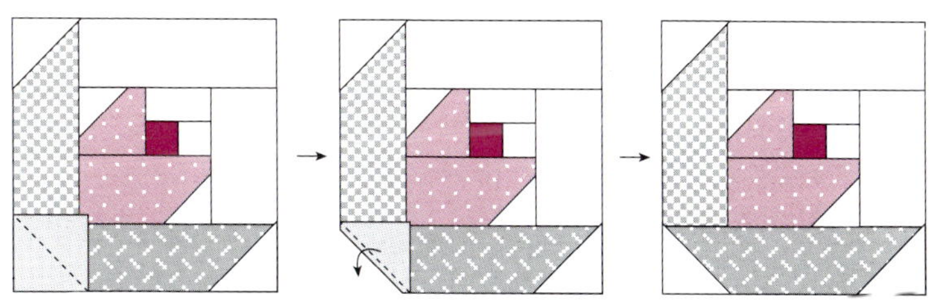

2. Strip piece 3"-wide white floral strips to top two sides of tulip, **Fig 11**. Repeat for all twelve tulips.

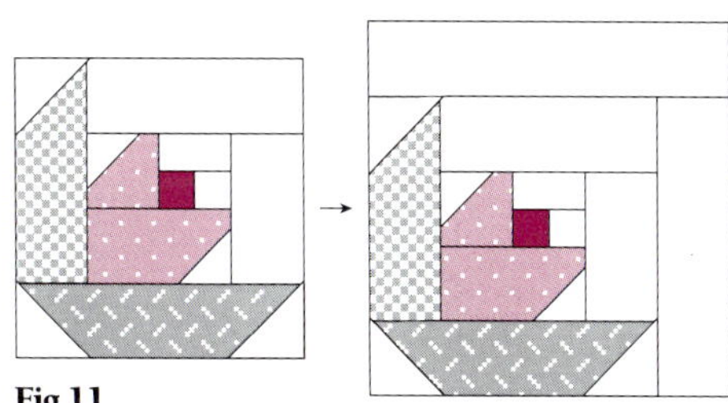

continued

3. Sew a second set of 3"-wide green print strips to lower sides of all twelve blocks, **Fig 12**. *Note: Use two different green prints in each block.*

4. Using the Stitch It, Snip It and Flip It technique, sew 3" white floral squares at tip of each leaf for Tulip Block B for central portion of quilt, **Fig 13**.

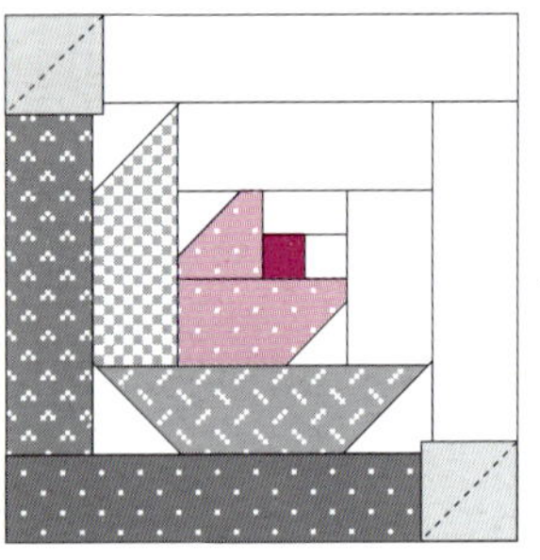 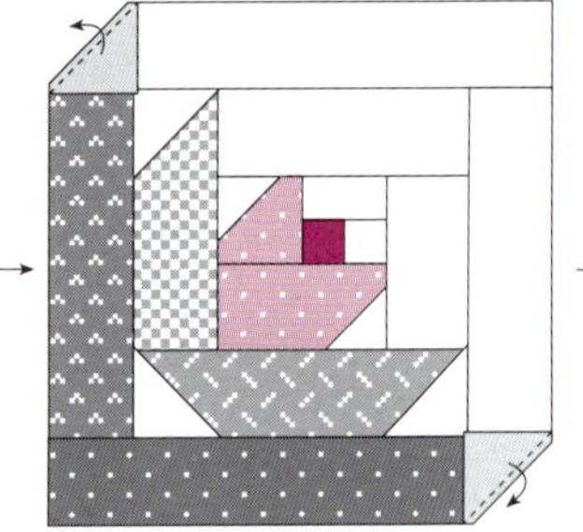

Fig 12

2. Place Tulip Block Bs and Tulip Block Cs as in **Fig 16**. Sew together in rows, then sew rows together.

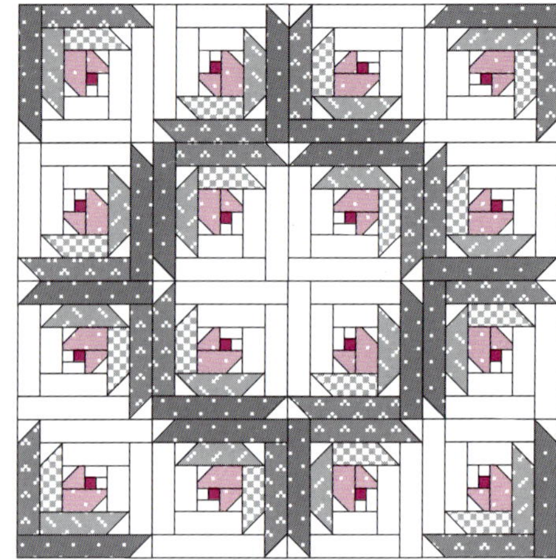

Fig 16

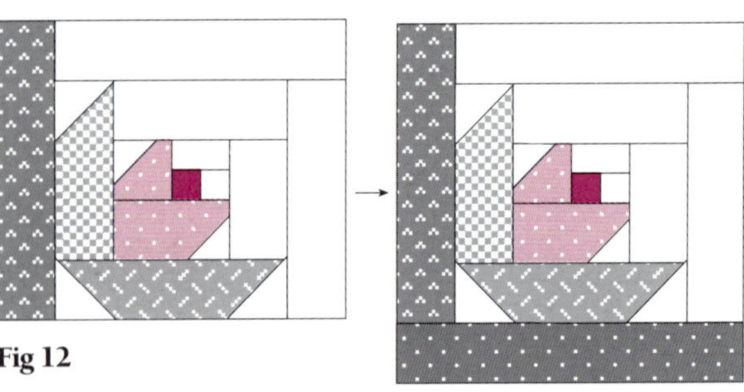

Fig 13

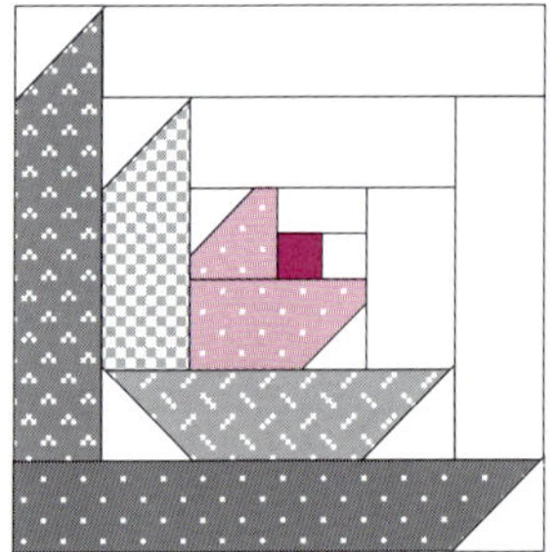

Tulip Block B

Making Tulip Block C

Strip piece 3"-wide white floral strip to top sides of reserved four Tulip Block As; add second set of 3"-wide green print strips and 3" white squares to complete Tulip Block C, **Fig 14**. *Note: This block is the same as Tulip Block B eliminating step 1 on page 19.*

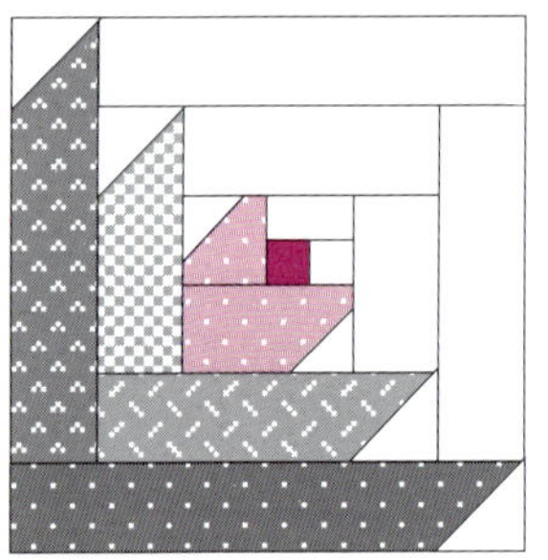

Fig 14   Tulip Block C

Assembling the Quilt

1. Sew 3" green print squares to corners of eight 5 1/2" x 10 1/2" rectangles using the Stitch It, Snip It and Flip It technique. Make four pairs as shown in **Fig 15**.

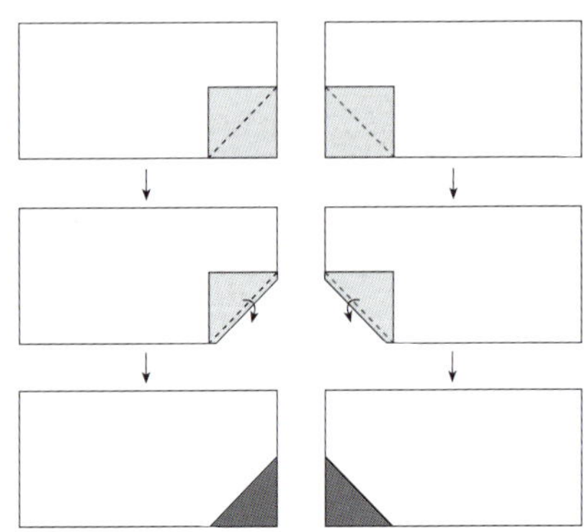

Fig 15

Make four pairs

3. For pieced border, sew Tulip Block A to opposite short sides of 10 1/2" x 30 1/2" white floral strip; sew pieced rectangle to each end, **Fig 17**. Repeat three more times. Sew pieced border to top and bottom of quilt.

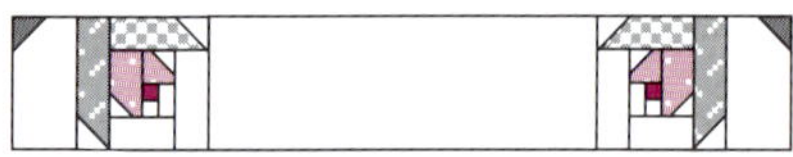

Fig 17

4. Sew another Tulip Block A to each end of remaining pieced strips noting position, **Fig 18**; sew to sides of quilt.

5. Sew green plaid and dk floral borders to the quilt referring to Simple Borders, page 9.

6. See the General Directions, pages 9 to 11, for finishing the quilt.

Fig 18

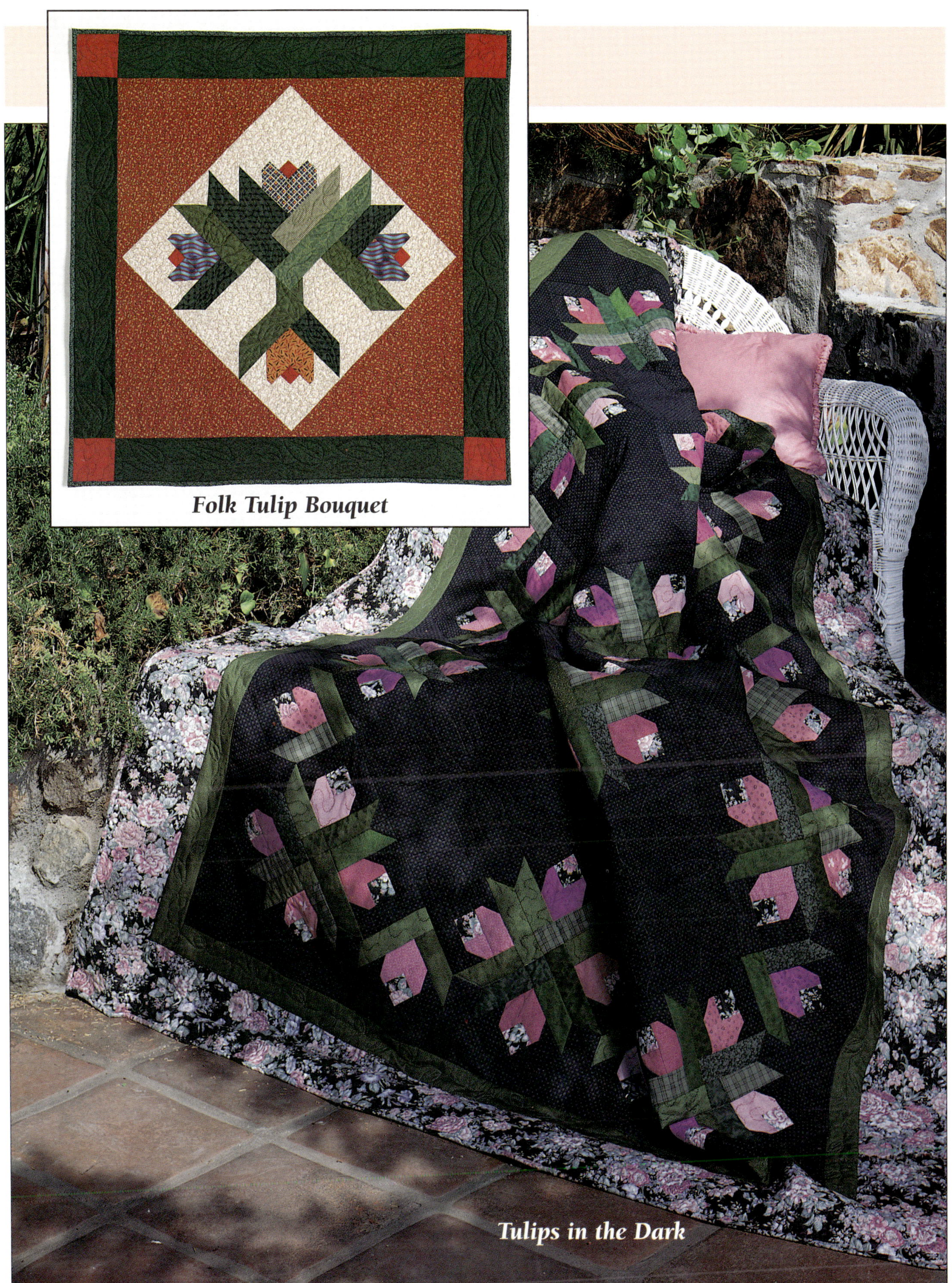

Folk Tulip Bouquet

Tulips in the Dark

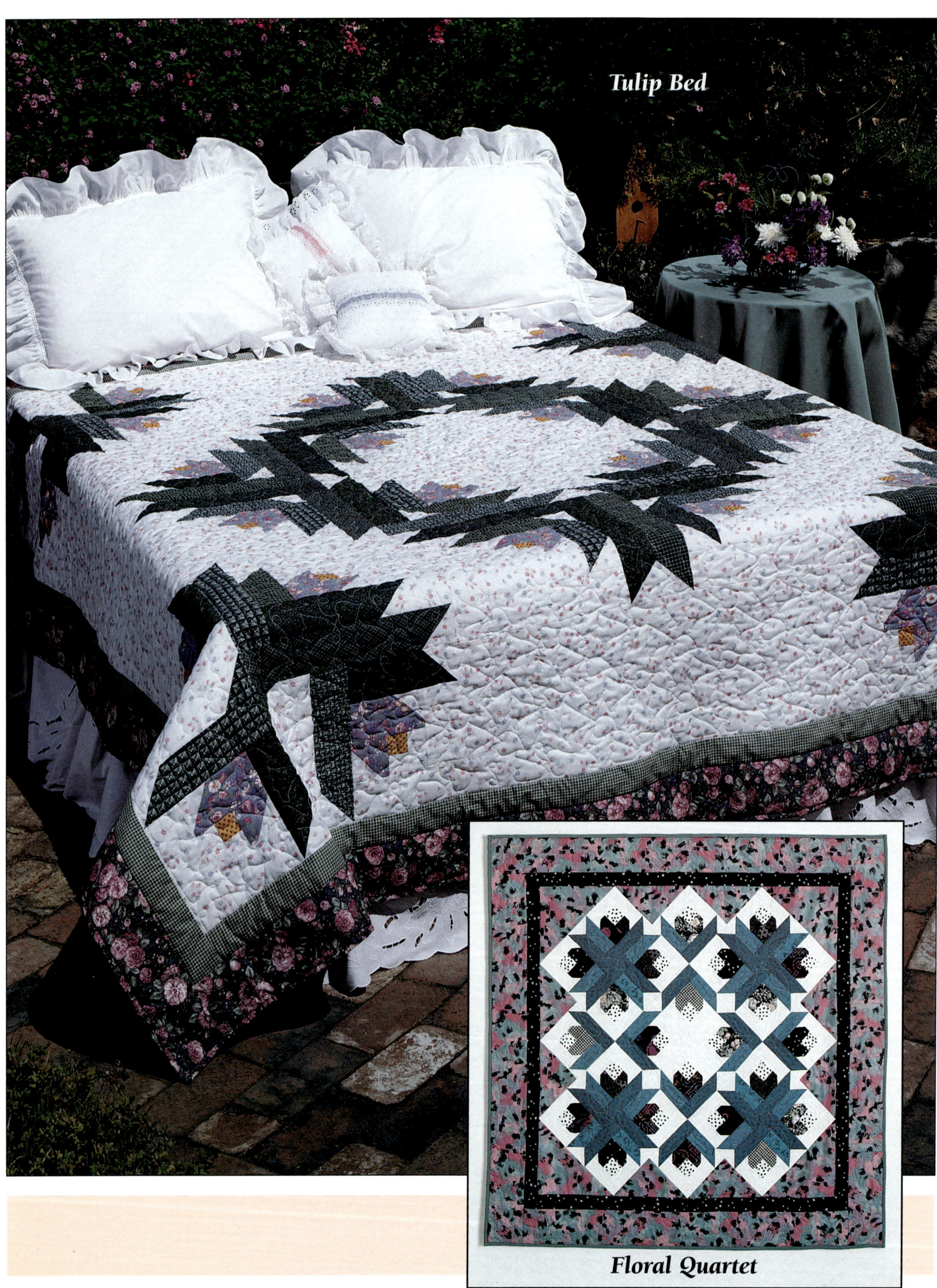
Tulip Bed
Floral Quartet

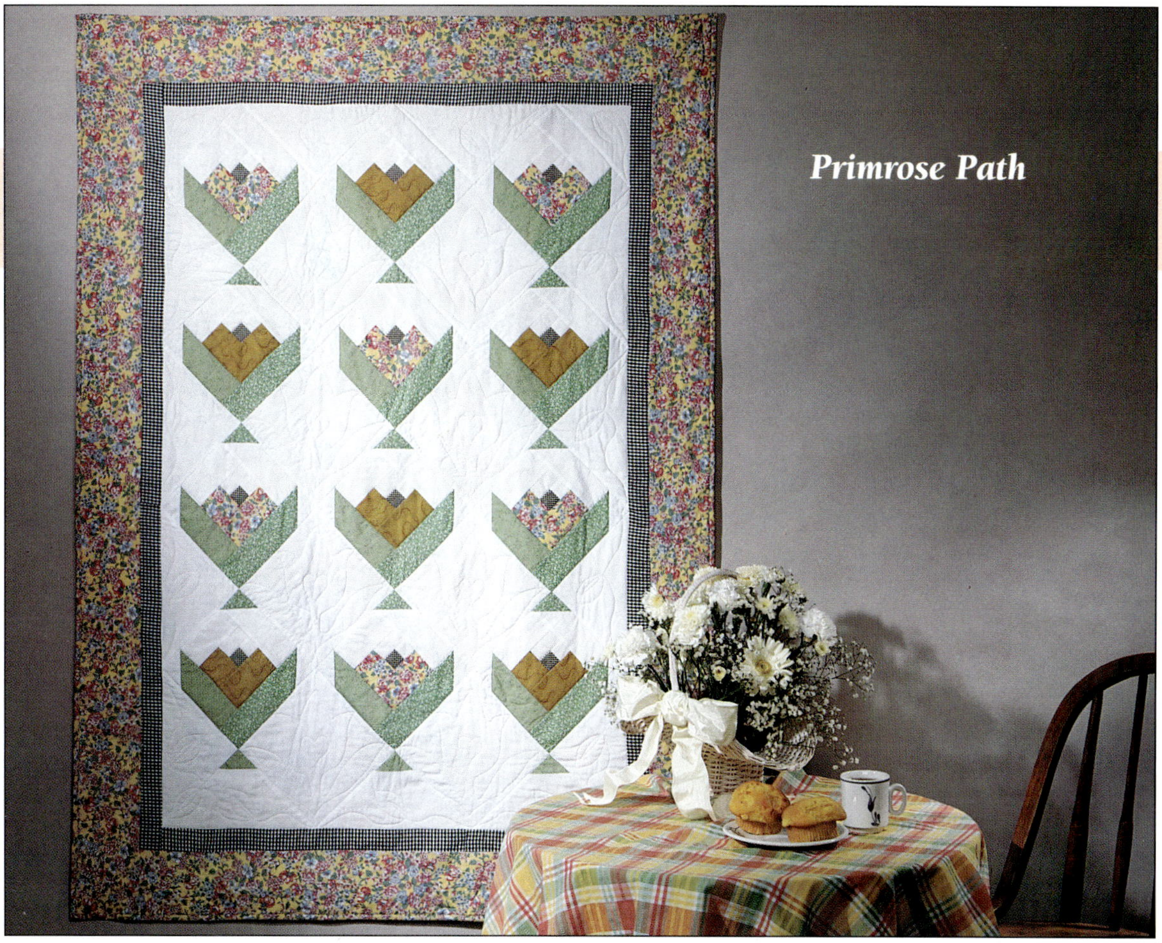

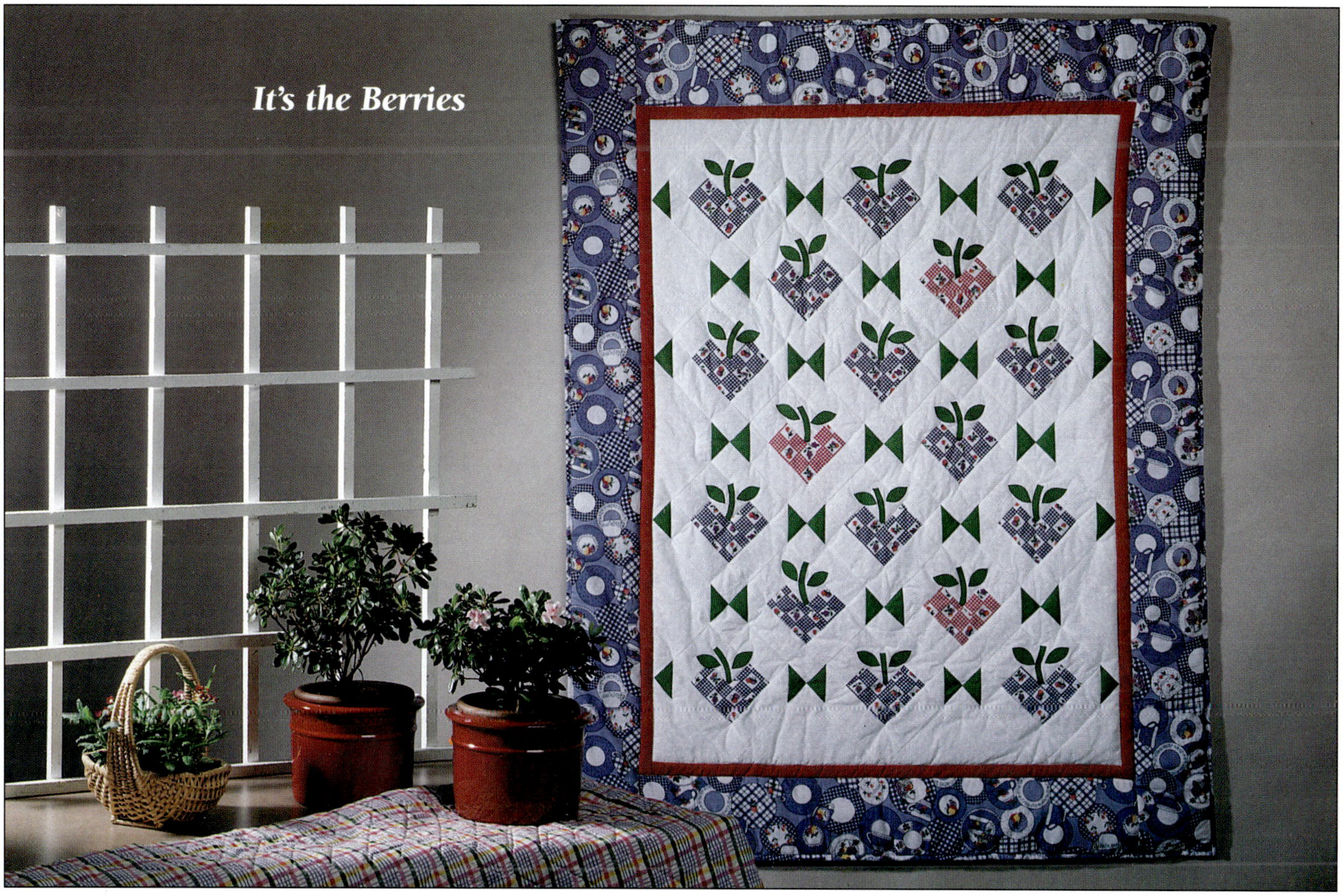

Primrose Path

It's the Berries

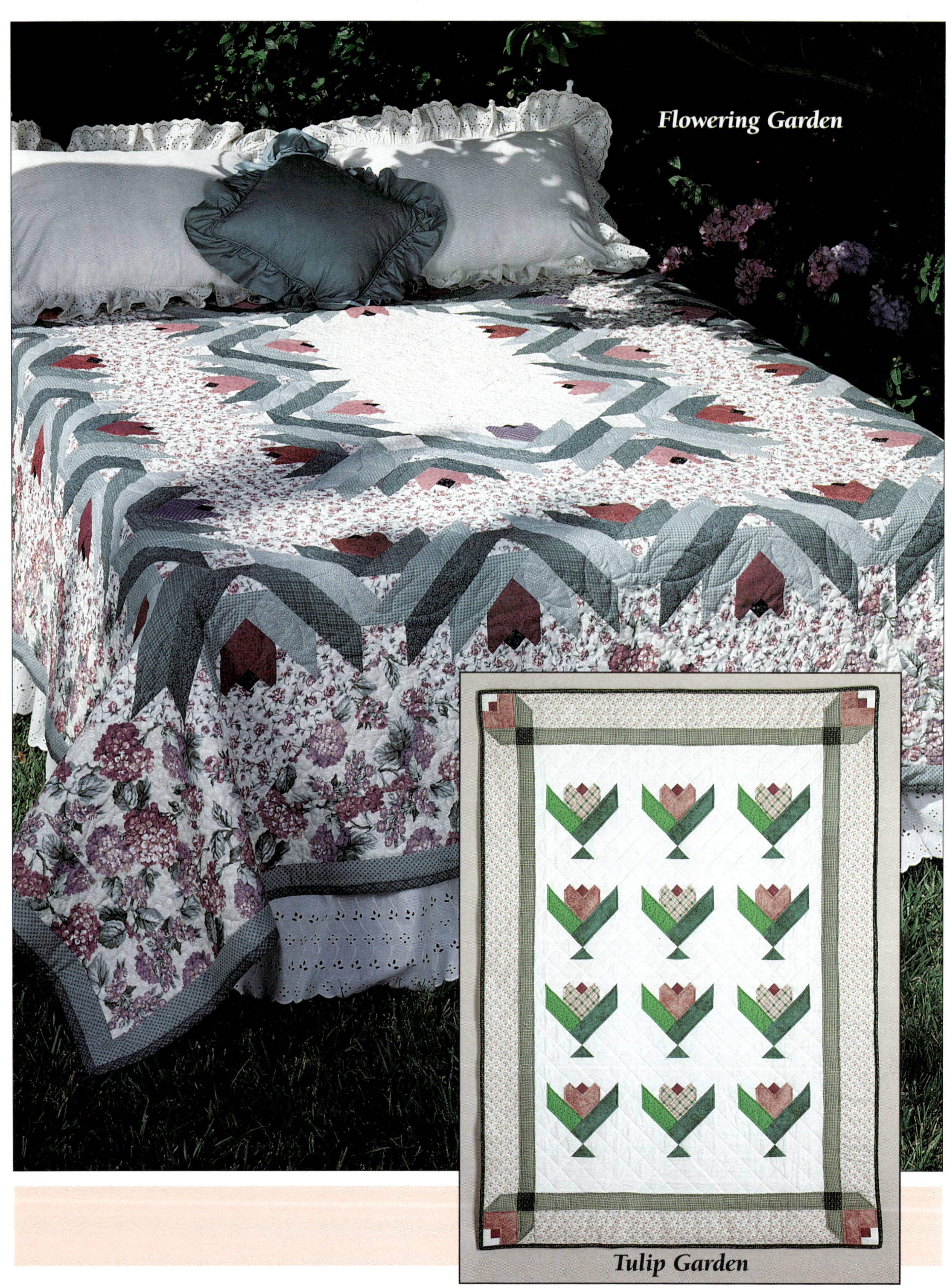

Tulip Garden

Folk Tulip Bouquet

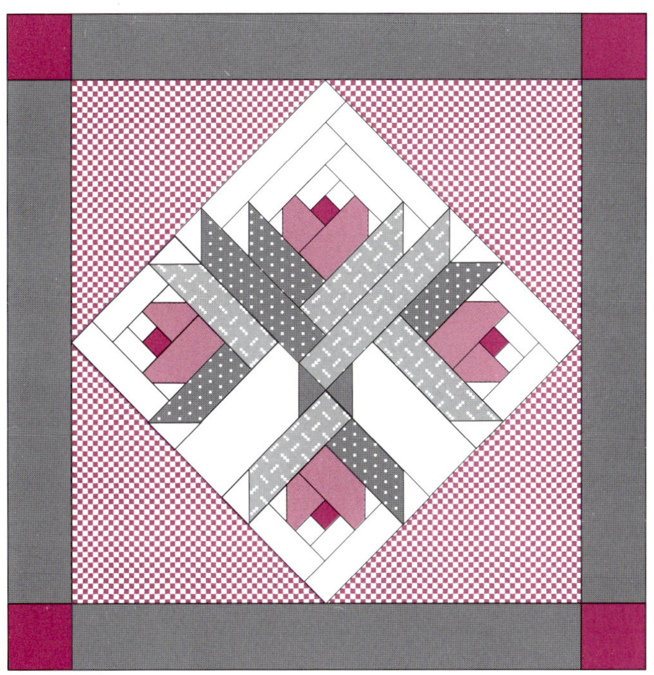

Shown in full color on page 21.

COLOR KEY

	Flower Fabrics
	Red Print
	Green Print 2
	Green Print 1
	Lt Tan
	Dk Red Floral
	Dk Green Print

APPROXIMATE SIZE: 34" x 34"

FINISHED BLOCK SIZES: 7 1/2" x 7 1/2" & 11" x 11"

You have probably already thought of ways to change many of the floral patterns in this book. Measurements CAN be changed and even mixed within the same quilt. This little project is designed to show you two ways it can be done, without adding anything complex. Try to discover the small changes.

Fabric Requirements:

1/8 yd flower fabric (or scraps of four different prints)
1/8 yd red print (or scraps) for centers and border squares
1/3 yd green fabrics (assorted green prints totaling 1/3 yd)
1/2 yd lt tan for background
1/2 yd dk red floral for corner triangles
1/2 yd dk green print for border
1/4 yd green print for binding
1 yd backing fabric
40" x 40" batting

Cutting Requirements:

four 2 1/2" x 4 1/2" rectangles, flower fabric
four 2 1/2" x 2 1/2" squares, flower fabric
four 1 1/2" x 1 1/2" squares red print (centers)
four 2 1/2"-wide strips, assorted green fabrics (leaves)
two 2 1/2" x 2 1/2" squares, green
one 1 1/2" x 18" strip lt tan (background)
two 2 "-wide strips, lt tan fabric (background)
six 1 3/4" x 1 3/4" squares, lt tan (for Tulip Block B)
two 1 1/4" x 1 1/4" squares, lt tan (for Tulip Block A)
ten 2 1/2" x 2 1/2" squares, lt tan
two 4" x 8" rectangles, lt tan (joining blocks)
two 15 1/2" x 15 1/2" squares, dk red floral (cut in half
   diagonally for corner triangles)
four 3 3/4" x 44" strips, dk green print (border)
four 2"-wide strips, green print (binding)

Instructions:

Making the Tulip Blocks

1. Strip piece 1 1/2" red print squares to 1 1/2" x 18" lt tan strip. Cut tan strip even with red print squares, **Fig 1**; finger press open.

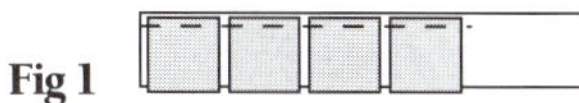

Fig 1

2. Strip piece units to remaining length of lt tan strip, **Fig 2**.

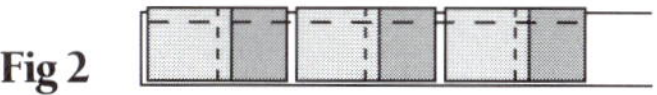

Fig 2

continued

3. Cut apart and finger press open, **Fig 3**.

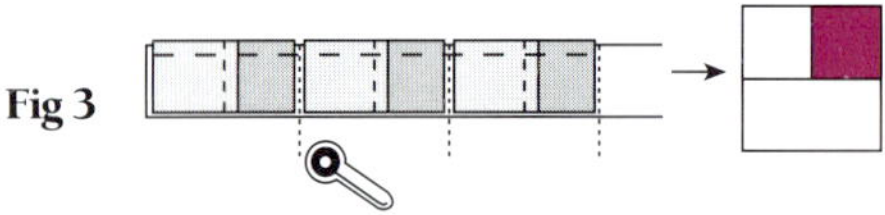

Fig 3

4. Chain stitch each unit to a 2 1/2" x 2 1/2" flower fabric square, **Fig 4**.

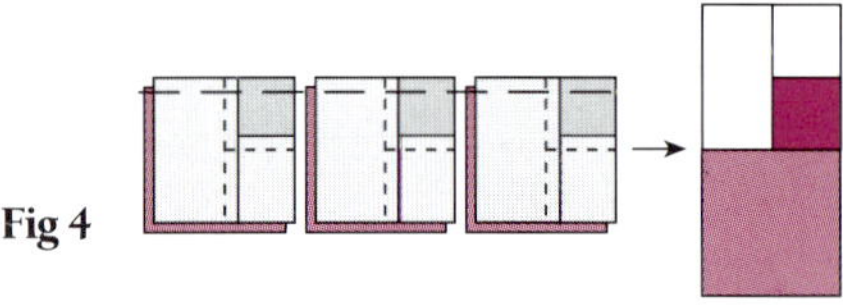

Fig 4

5. Chain stitch a 2 1/2" x 4 1/2" flower fabric rectangle to each of these units, **Fig 5**.

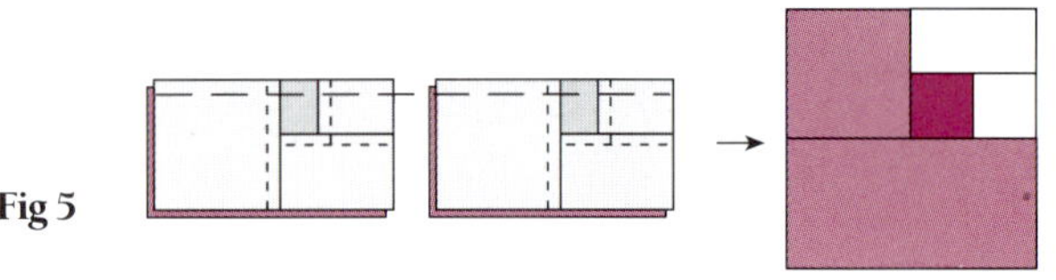

Fig 5

6. Using the Stitch It, Snip It and Flip It technique, page 8, sew 1 1/4" lt tan squares to sides of one flower for Tulip Block A, **Fig 6**. Sew 1 3/4" lt tan squares to remaining three flowers for Tulip Block B, **Fig 7**.

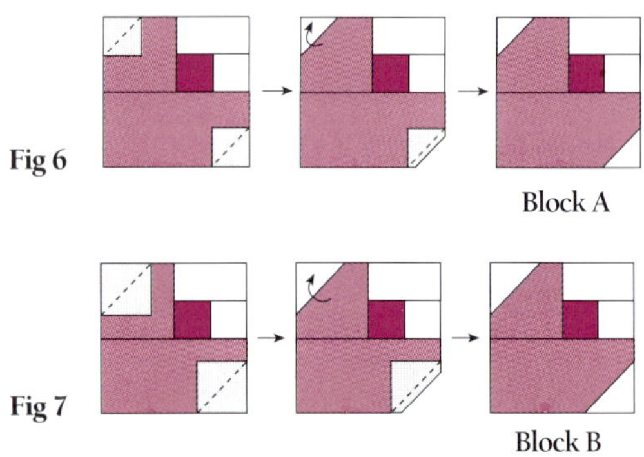

Fig 6

Block A

Fig 7

Block B

7. Strip piece 2"-wide lt tan strips to two top sides of Tulip Blocks A and B; cut apart and press with an iron, **Fig 8**.

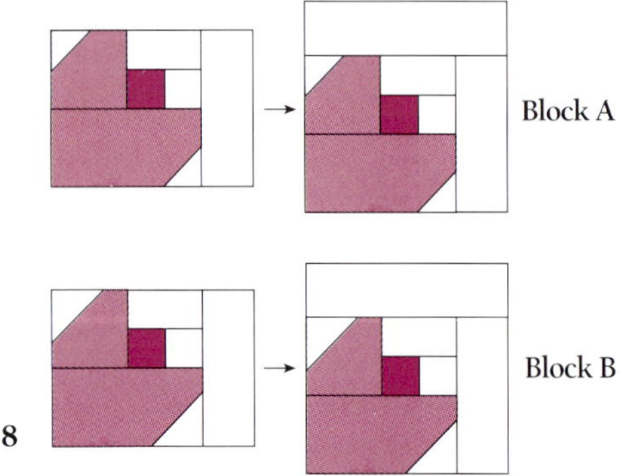

Block A

Block B

Fig 8

8. Sew assorted green print strips to two lower sides of tulips; press, **Fig 9**.

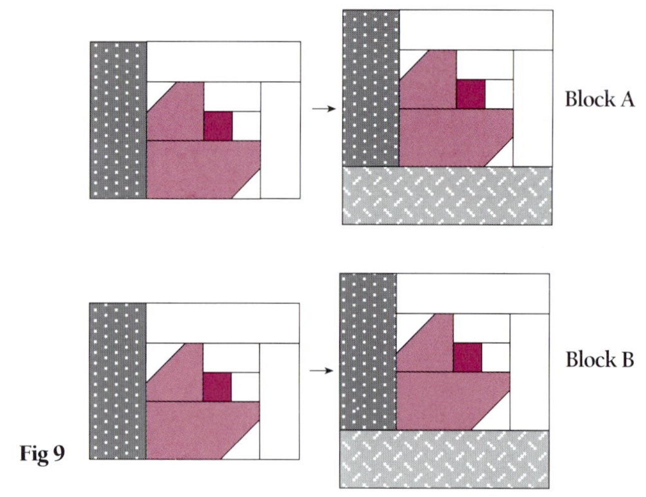

Block A

Block B

Fig 9

9. Using the Stitch It, Snip It and Flip It technique, sew 2 1/2" lt tan squares to tips of leaves, **Fig 10**; press.

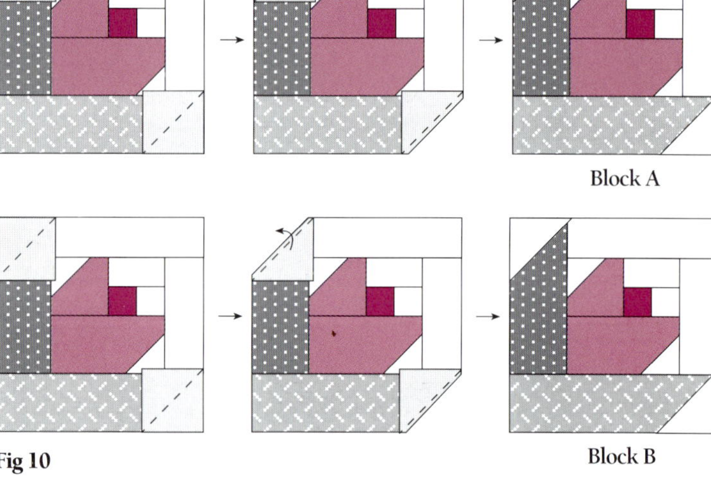

Block A

Fig 10

Block B

10. Strip piece 2"-wide lt tan strips to two top sides of Tulip Block A, **Fig 11**.

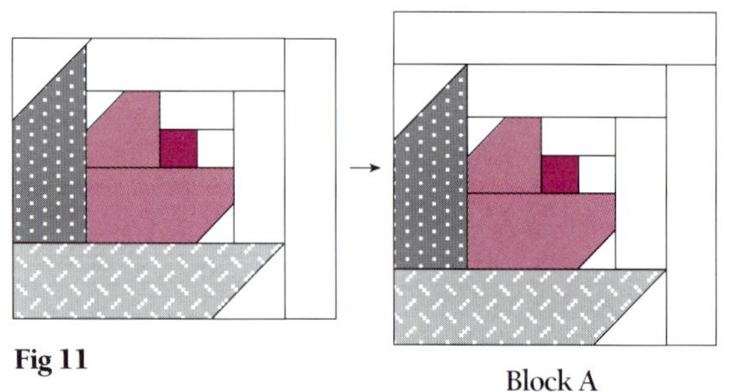

Fig 11

Block A

11. Sew green strips to two lower sides of Tulip Block A using one dk green strip, then one med green print strip, **Fig 12**.

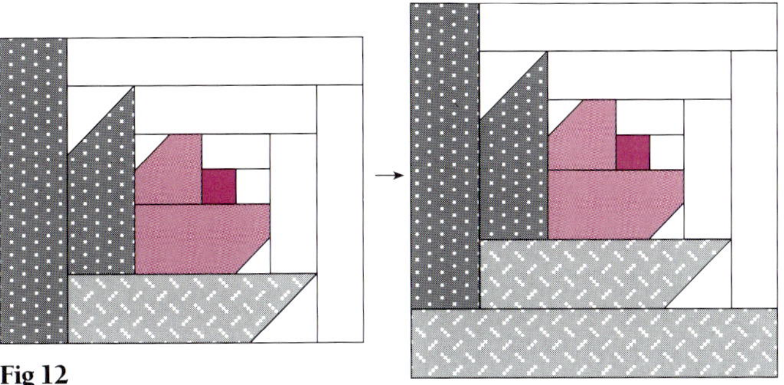

Fig 12

12. Sew 2 1/2" lt tan squares to tips of leaves using the Stitch It, Snip It and Flip It technique to complete Tulip Block A, **Fig 13**.

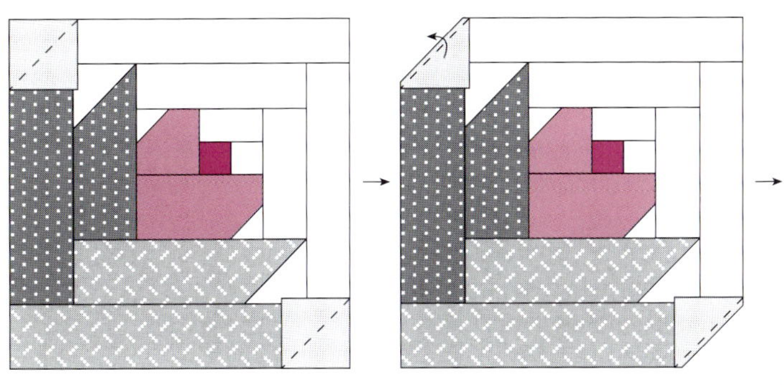
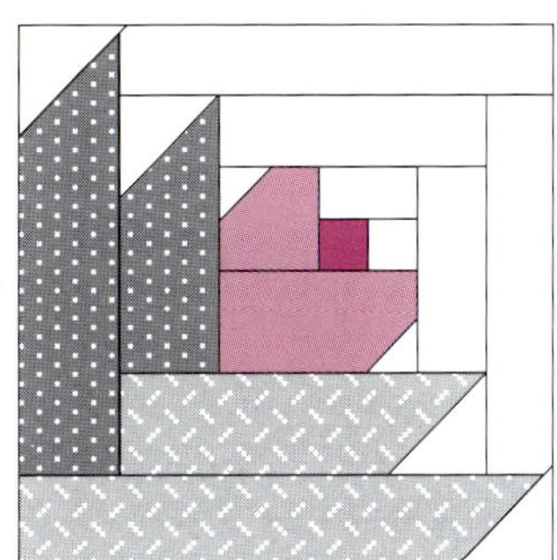

Fig 13

Tulip Block A

13. Sew dk green square to corner of a 4" x 8" lt tan rectangle, using the Stitch It, Snip It and Flip It technique. Repeat, sewing dk green square to opposite corner as shown, **Fig 14**.

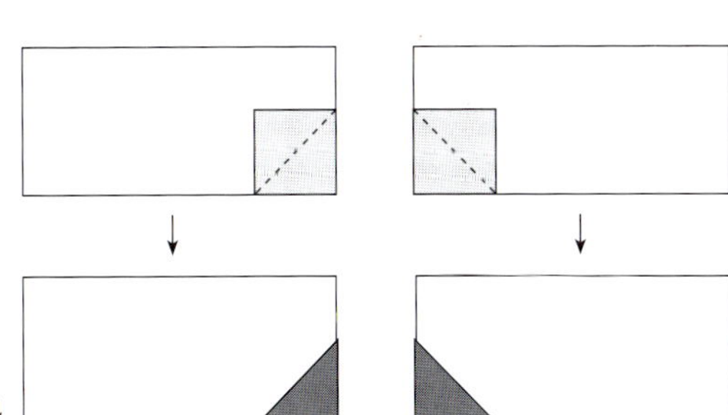

Fig 14

Assembling the Quilt

1. Arrange Tulip Blocks (Block A at top), pieced rectangles and corner triangles, **Fig 15**; sew together.

2. Sew borders to quilt referring to Borders with Corner Squares, page 9.

3. Refer to General Directions, pages 9 to 11, for finishing the quilt.

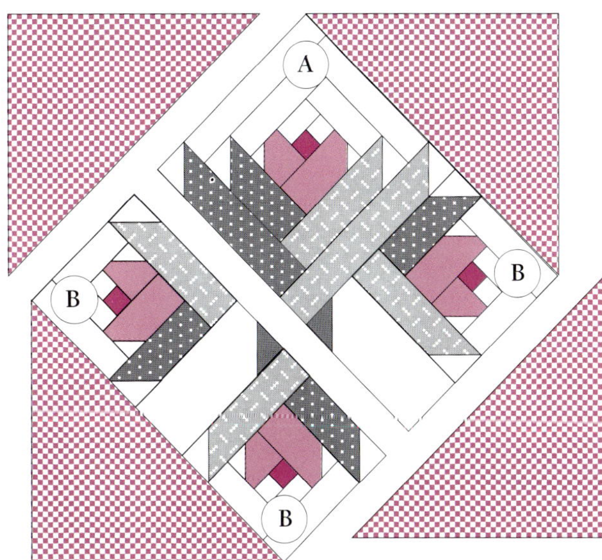

Fig 15

27

Windblown Tulips

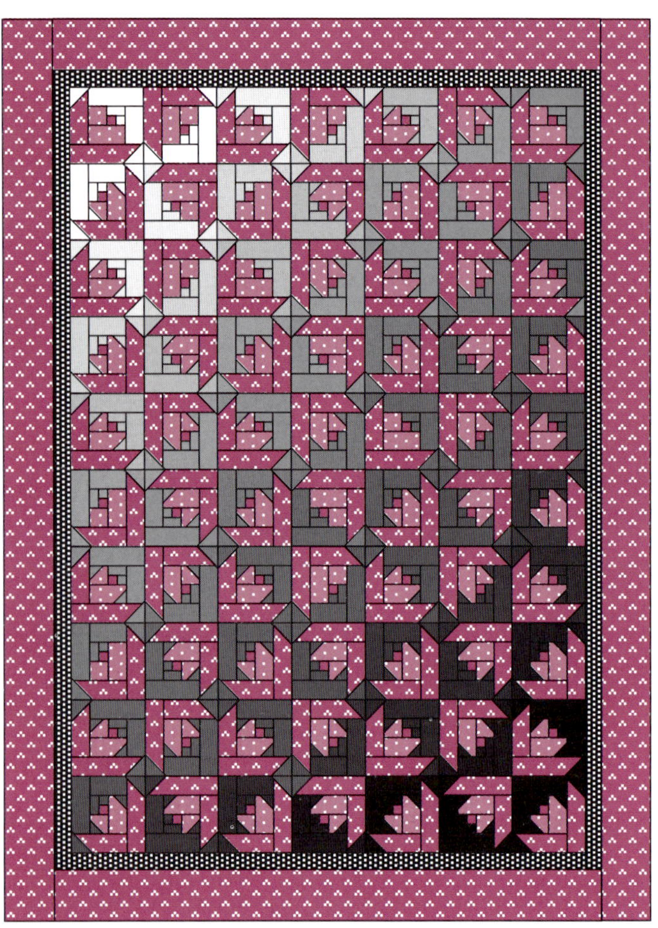

Shown in full color on front and back cover.

COLOR KEY

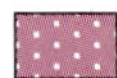 Assorted lt, bright fabrics

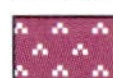 Green Print

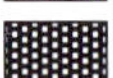 Black

APPROXIMATE SIZE: 52" x 72"

FINISHED BLOCK SIZE: 6" x 6"

There are 70 six-inch blocks in this dramatic lap quilt. Don't let the number of blocks keep you from making this quilt. The easy-to-make Tulip pattern is the same throughout. The variety of colors in the tulips and the changes in the background fabric color values will keep you interested and on your toes!

All of the fabrics in this quilt were purchased right off the shelf from several fabric stores. None was hand-dyed. It may be a challenge to find the 14 background fabrics—but you know the search will be a lot of fun.

The background fabrics are labeled with letters. The lightest color values are A, B, C and D with the color values becoming progressively darker. The darkest of the color values in this quilt are L, M and N.

Fabric Requirements:

3/4 yd assorted light, bright fabrics for tulips (each tulip requires 2" x 5 1/2")

1/4 yd total of assorted fabric scraps for tulip centers

1 1/4 yds green print for leaves

2 1/4 yds total of assorted background fabrics progressing from light to dark values:

A - 2" x 44" (3 blocks)	H - 1/4 yd (7 blocks)
B - 2" x 44" (3 blocks)	I - 1/4 yd (7 blocks)
C - 1/8 yd (4 blocks)	J - 1/8 yd (6 blocks)
D - 1/8 yd (5 blocks)	K - 1/8 yd (5 blocks)
E - 1/8 yd (6 blocks)	L - 1/8 yd (4 blocks)
F - 1/4 yd (7 blocks)	M - 2" x 44" (3 blocks)
G - 1/4 yd (7 blocks)	N - 2" x 44" (3 blocks)

3/4 yd black solid for first border

1 1/4 yds green print for second border and binding

2 1/8 yds 60"-wide quilt backing

twin size batting

Cutting Requirements:

70 - 1 1/4" x 1 1/4" squares, assorted scraps (centers)
70 - 2" x 2" squares, assorted light, bright (tulips)
70 - 2" x 3 1/2" rectangles, assorted light, bright (tulips)
twenty 2"-wide strips, green print (leaves)
106 - 1 1/2" x 1 1/2" squares (background)
    six, Fabric A
    six, Fabric B
    eight, Fabric C
    ten, Fabric D
    twelve, Fabric E
    fourteen, Fabric F
    fourteen, Fabric G
    fourteen, Fabric H
    fourteen, Fabric I
    twelve, Fabric J
    ten, Fabric K
    eight, Fabric L
    six, Fabric M
    six, Fabric N
one 1 1/4" x 10" strip, Fabrics A, B, M, N
one 1 1/4" x 14" strip, Fabrics C and L
one 1 1/4" x 22" strip, Fabrics D and K
one 1 1/4" x 30" strip, Fabrics E and J
one 1 1/4" x 38" strip, Fabrics F, G, H, I
one 2" x 44" strip, Fabrics A, B, C, L, M, N
two 2" x 44" strips, Fabrics D, E, F, G, H, I, J, K
140 squares 2" x 2", assorted background
    six 2" squares each, Fabrics A, B, M, N
    eight 2" squares each, Fabrics C and L
    ten 2" squares each, Fabrics D and K
    twelve 2" squares each, Fabrics E and J
    fourteen 2" squares each, Fabrics F, G, H, and I
six 1 3/4"-wide strips, black solid (first border)
six 4 1/2"-wide strips, green print (second border)
six 2"-wide strips, green print (binding)

Instructions:

Making the Blocks

1. See block placement and number of blocks required from each background fabric, A through N, in **Fig 1**. *Note: Be sure to use the same background fabric throughout a single block.*

A	A	B	C	D	E	F
A	B	C	D	E	F	G
B	C	D	E	F	G	H
C	D	E	F	G	H	I
D	E	F	G	H	I	J
E	F	G	H	I	J	K
F	G	H	I	J	K	L
G	H	I	J	K	L	M
H	I	J	K	L	M	N
I	J	K	L	M	N	N

Fig 1

2. Strip piece 1 1/4" center squares to 1 1/4"-wide Fabric A background strip; cut apart with scissors. Open and finger press, **Fig 2**.

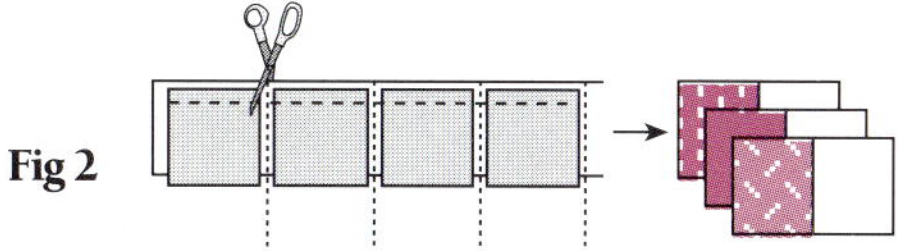

3. Strip piece these units to the remainder of the 1 1/4"-wide background fabric; cut apart with scissors and finger press open, **Fig 3**.

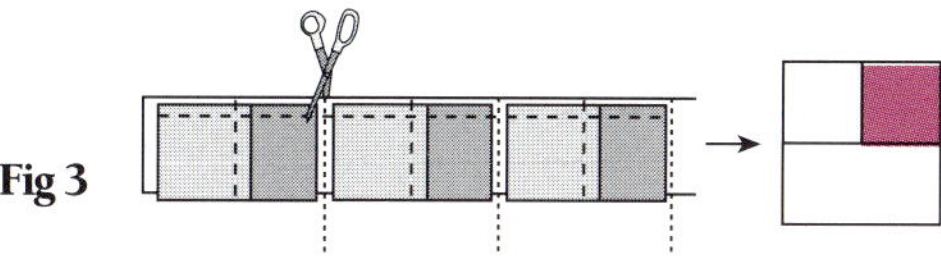

4. Sew center unit to 2" tulip square; finger press open, **Fig 4**.

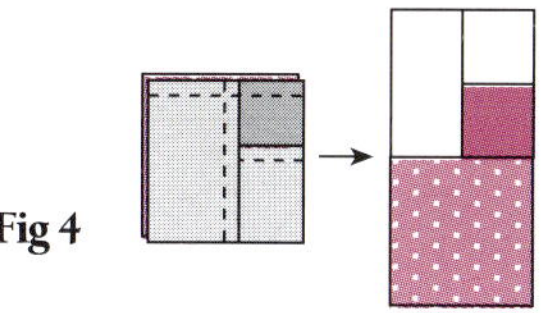

5. Next, sew 2" x 3 1/2" tulip rectangle to unit. Finger press open, **Fig 5**.

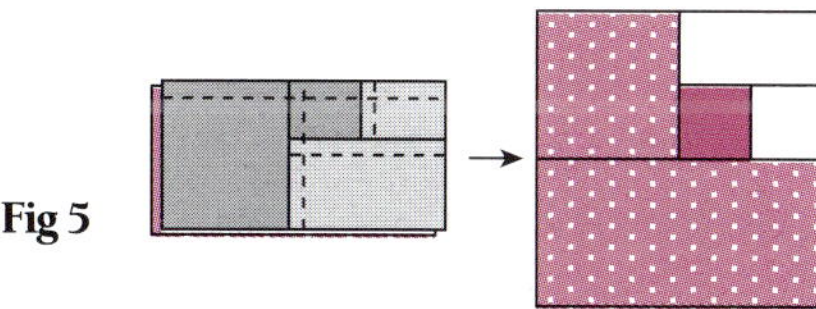

6. Repeat steps 2 to 5 for each background fabric referring to **Fig 1** for number of blocks that uses each background fabric.

7. Sew 1 1/2" background squares to corners of tulips using the Stitch It, Snip It and Flip It technique, page 8, **Fig 6**. *Note: You may choose to omit the 1 1/2" background squares on some blocks; the photographed quilt has 17 blocks without them. These tulips are "open" or "windblown."*

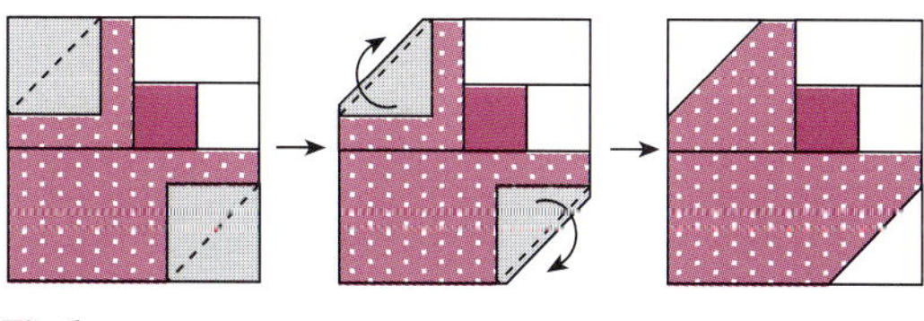

continued

8. Strip piece matching 2"-wide background strips to top two sides of all tulips, **Fig 7**. Press seams to one side with an iron.

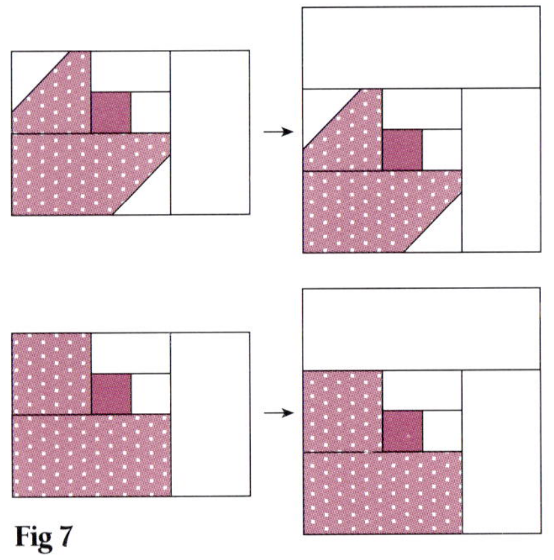

Fig 7

9. Strip piece 2"-wide leaf fabric strips to two lower sides of tulips, **Fig 8**.

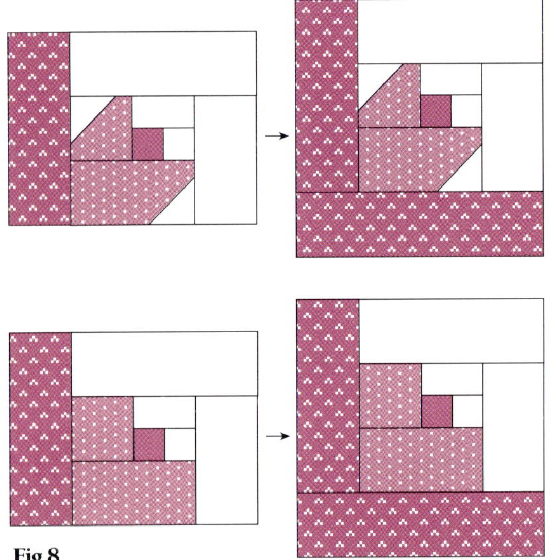

Fig 8

10. Using the Stitch It, Snip It and Flip It technique, sew 2" background squares to corners of leaves; press with an iron, **Fig 9**.

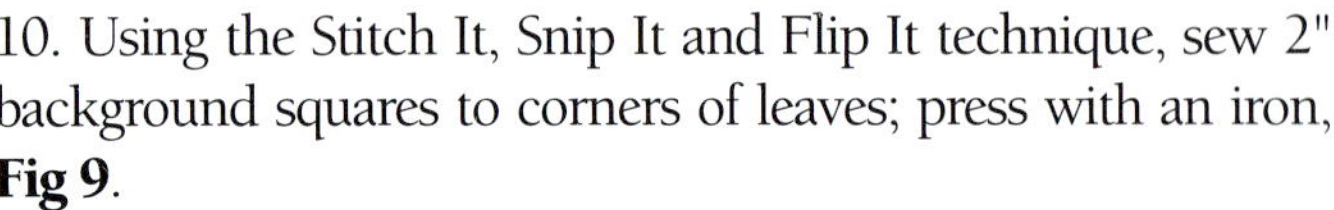

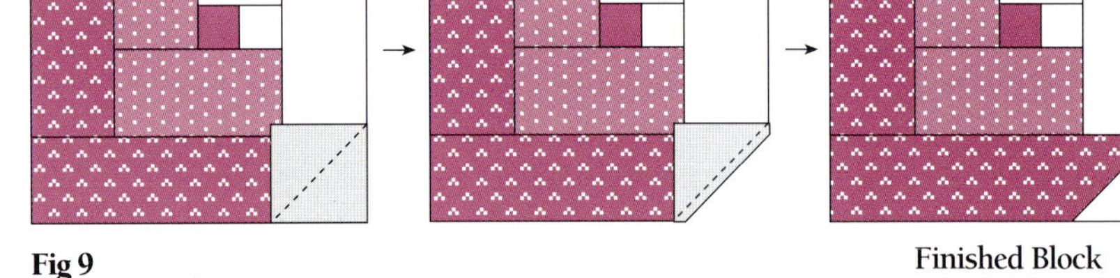

Fig 9

11. Complete all 70 blocks with the appropriate background fabrics.

Assembling the Quilt

1. Place blocks according to layout (page 28) and **Fig 1** (page 29). Note that direction of tulips alternates in each row.

2. Sew the border to quilt referring to Simple Borders, page 9.

3. Refer to General Directions, pages 9 to 11, to finish the quilt.

Tulips in the Dark

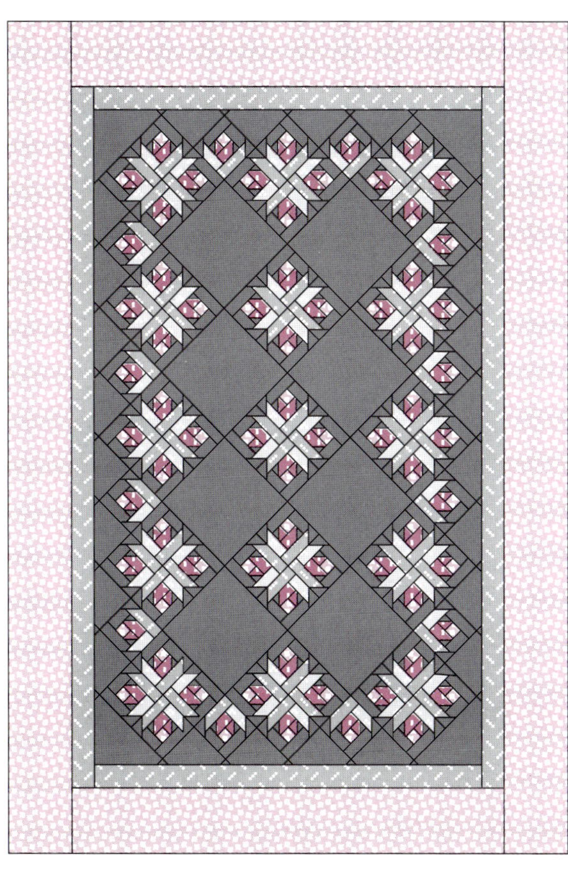

Shown in full color on page 21.

COLOR KEY

- Pink Print
- Floral Print
- Med Lt Green
- Med Dk Green
- Dk Print

APPROXIMATE SIZE: 64" x 95"

FINISHED BLOCK SIZES: 6" SUB-BLOCKS & 12" BLOCKS

This day bed size quilt will dress up any studio or guest bedroom. The simplified center makes this floral design very quick to piece. The dark background makes it dramatic.

Fabric Requirements:

2/3 yd pink print for flowers (fabric may be mixed—each flower needs a 2" x 7" strip)

1/4 yd floral print for centers
(**Note:** *The print background color should match the background fabric.*)

3/4 yd med lt green for leaves

3/4 yd med dk green for leaves

3 yds dk print for background

5/8 yd med dk green for first border

2 1/4 yds floral print for second border and binding.
(**Note:** *In the photographed model the flower center fabric and the second border fabrics were the same.*)

5 1/2 yds 44"-wide fabric for backing

twin size batting

Cutting Requirements:

Note: *Cut all strips along the crosswise grain.*

four 2" strips each, floral fabric (centers)

2"-wide strips, pink print (if using scraps allow 7" per flower)

ten 2"-wide strips, med lt and med dk green (leaves)

twenty 2"-wide strips, dk print (background)

144 - 1 1/4" x 1 1/4" squares dk print (background)

four 2"-wide strips, dk print (background)

144 - 2" x 2" squares dk print (background)

eight 12 1/2" x 12 1/2" squares dk print (skip blocks)

six 9 1/2" x 9 1/2" squares, dk print (cut diagonally in quarters for finishing triangles, **Fig 1**)

two 9 1/4" x 9 1/4" squares, dk print (cut diagonally in half for the corners, **Fig 2**)

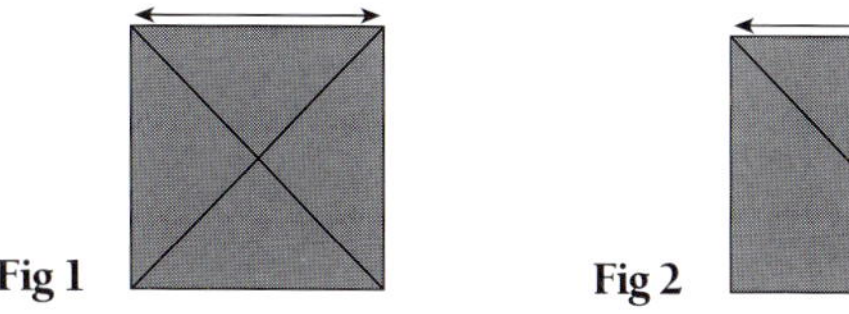

seven 2 1/2"-wide strips, med green (first border)

eight 6"-wide strips, floral fabric (second border)

eight 2 1/4"-wide strips, floral fabric (binding)

continued

Instructions:

Making the Sub-block Units

1. Strip piece 2"-wide floral print center strip to a 2"-wide pink print strip. Cut apart into 2"-wide units; finger press open, **Fig 3**.

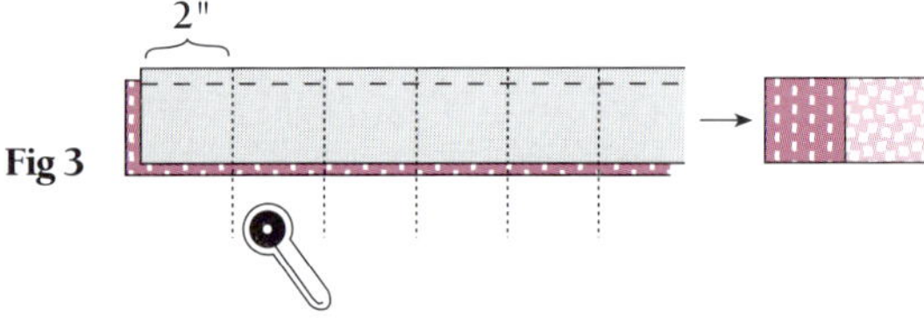

Fig 3

2. Strip piece these units to 2"-wide pink print strips (or matching flower print if using scraps); cut apart and press open, **Fig 4**.

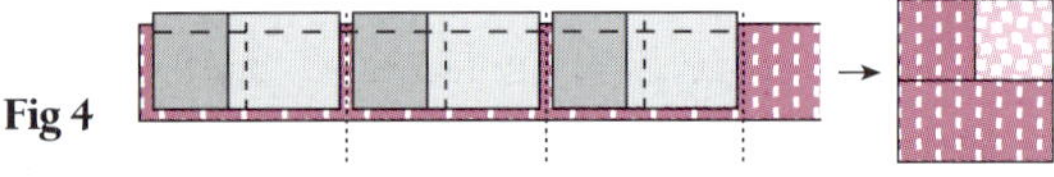

Fig 4

3. Using the Stitch It, Snip It and Flip It technique, page 8, add the 1 1/4" x 1 1/4" dk print background squares to the sides of the flowers, **Fig 5**; press.

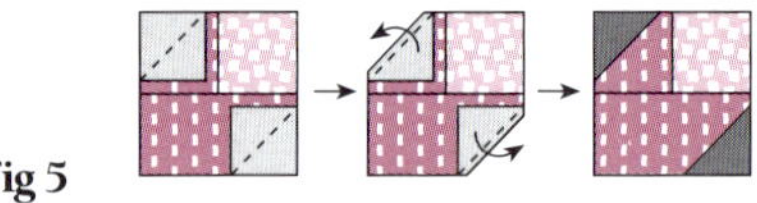

Fig 5

4. Strip piece 2"-wide dk print background strips to top two sides of flowers, **Fig 6**; press.

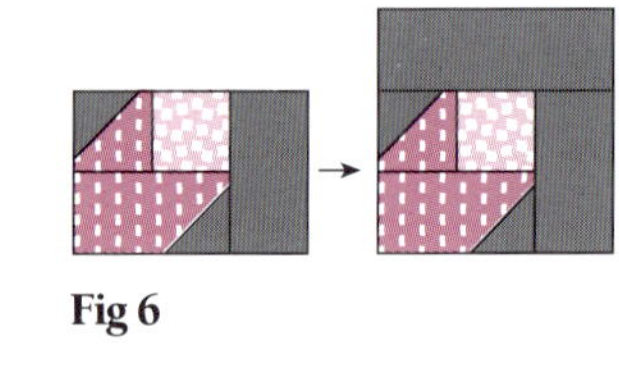

Fig 6

5. Strip piece med lt green strip to flower units; then add med dk green strip, **Fig 7**. Press toward the outside of unit after each addition.

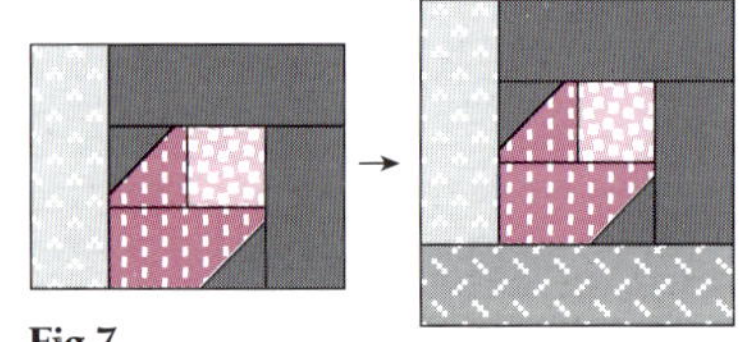

Fig 7

6. Using the Stitch It, Snip It and Flip It technique sew 2" x 2" dk print squares to ends of leaves, **Fig 8**; press. Make 72 Sub-block Units

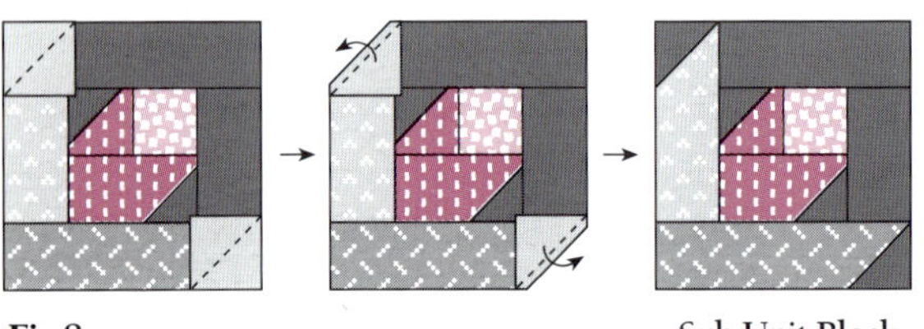

Fig 8

Sub-Unit Block

Making the Large Tulip Blocks

1. Square the Sub-block Units if necessary. They should measure 6 1/2" x 6 1/2" before assembly. Set aside twelve Sub-block Units.

2. Piece together four Sub-block Units to create a large block, **Fig 9**; press. Repeat for a total of fifteen Large Tulip Blocks.

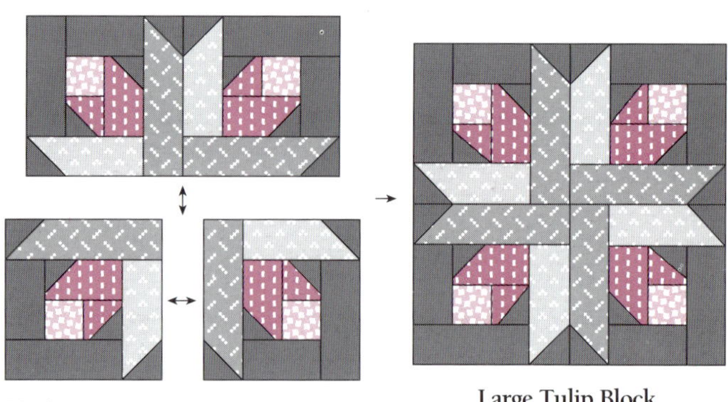

Fig 9

Large Tulip Block

Assembling the Quilt

1. Sew a dk print finishing triangle to adjacent sides of a reserved sub-block unit, **Fig 10**. Repeat for a total of twelve Pieced Finishing Triangles.

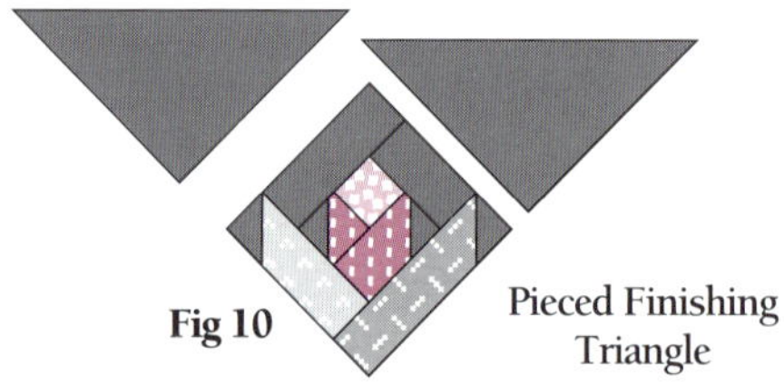

Fig 10

Pieced Finishing Triangle

2. Place Large Tulip Blocks, Skip Blocks, Pieced Finishing Triangles and corner triangles as in **Fig 11**; sew together in rows, then sew rows together.

3. Sew borders to quilt referring to Simple Borders, page 9.

4. See the General Directions, pages 9 to 11, for finishing the quilt.

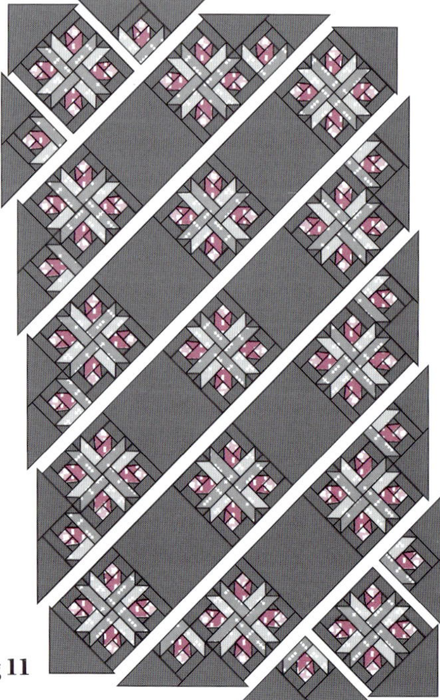

Fig 11

Floral Quartet

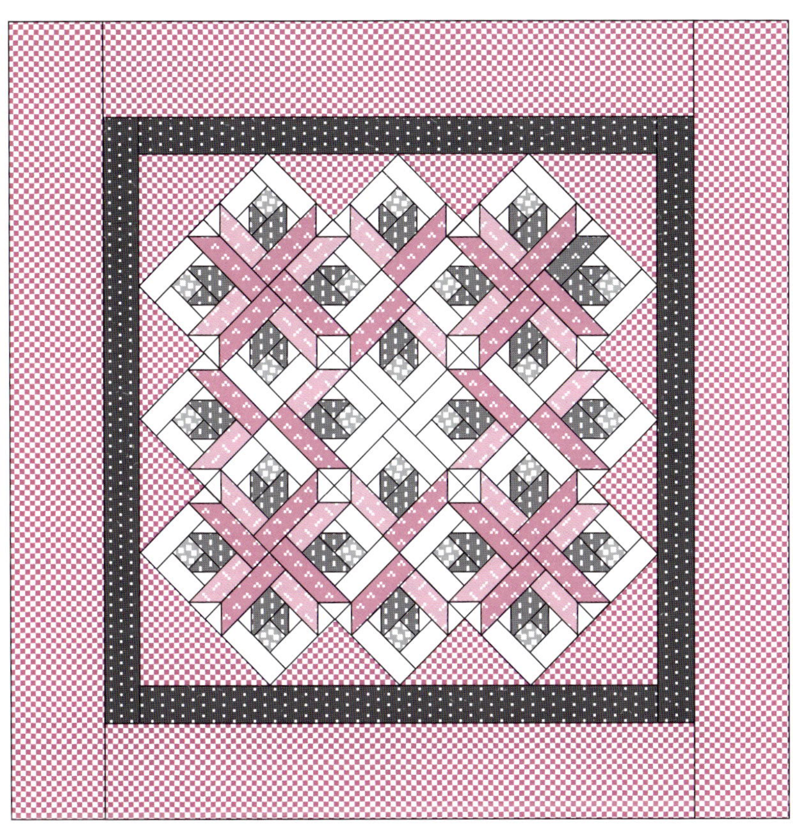

Shown in full color on page 22.

APPROXIMATE SIZE 45" x 45"

FINISHED BLOCK SIZE: 6" x 6"

A simplified center makes this floral the quickest quilt in the book. The fabric for the flowers in the contemporary medallion are all left over, but treasured 2"-wide strips from other piecing projects. Even the teal green leaf strips were picked up from the studio floor. Maybe we should rename the quilt the Just Enough Scraps Quilt.

Fabric Requirements:

1/8 yd black polka dot print for centers
1/4 yd black print (or 2" x 7" black print
   scraps) for flowers
1/3 yd med teal for leaves
1/3 yd dk teal for leaves
2/3 yd white for background
1/4 yd black star print for first border
1 yd dk print for finishing triangles and
   second border
1/3 yd solid med teal for binding
1 5/8 yds 44"-wide fabric for backing
47" x 47" batting

COLOR KEY

 Black Polka Dot

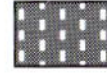 Black Print

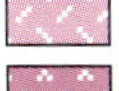 Med Teal

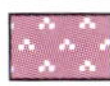 Dk Teal

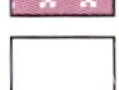 White Background

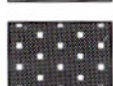 Black Star Print

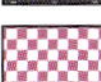 Dk Print

Cutting Requirements:

one 2"-wide strip, black polka dot print (centers)
four 2"-wide strips, black print (if using scraps allow 7"
   per flower)
four 2"-wide strips, med teal (leaves)
four 2"-wide strips, dk teal (leaves)
eight 2"-wide strips, white (background)
48 - 1 1/4" x 1 1/4" squares, white (background)
48 - 2" x 2" squares, white (background)
four 2"-wide strips, black star print (first border)
five 4 1/2"-wide strips dark print (second border)
five 2"-wide strips, med teal

continued

two 9 1/2" x 9 1/2" squares, dark print (cut diagonally
   into quarters for finishing triangles, **Fig 1**)
two 9 1/4" x 9 1/4" squares, dark print (cut in half
   diagonally for corners, **Fig 2**)

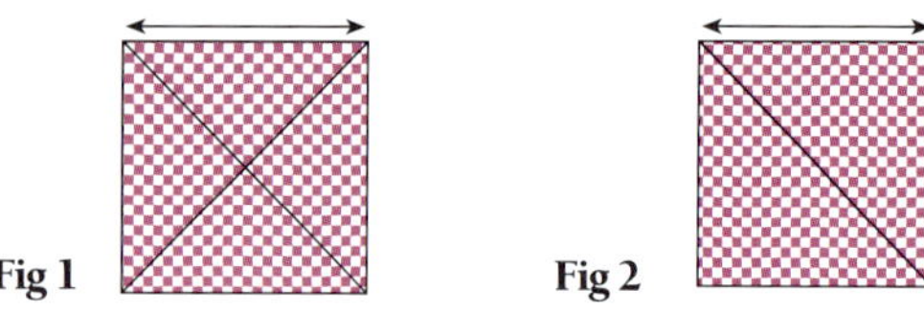

Fig 1   Fig 2

Instructions:

Making the Flower Block

1. Strip piece the black polka dot print center strip to a
flower strip.

2. Rotary cut apart into 2" wide units. Finger press open,
Fig 3.

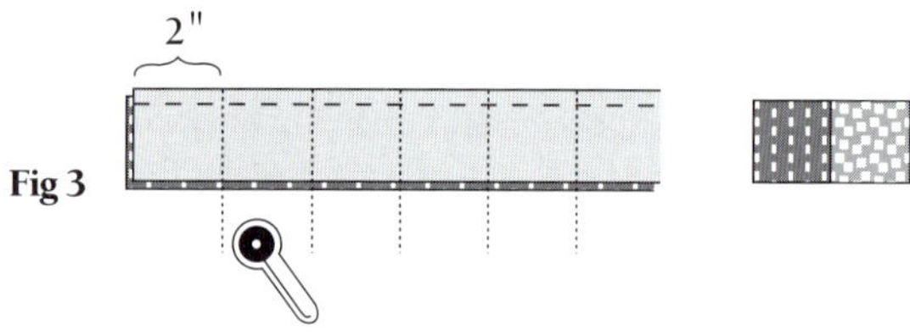

Fig 3

3. Strip these units to matching flower fabric strips. Cut apart
and press open, **Fig 4**.

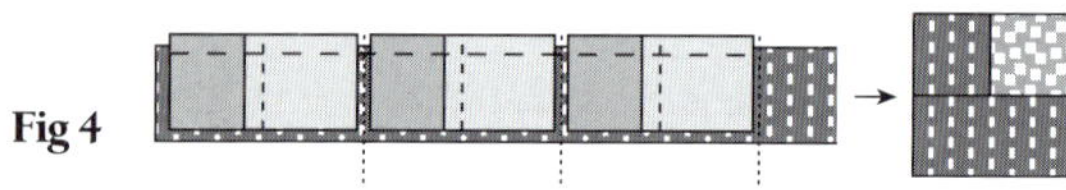

Fig 4

4. Using the Stitch It, Snip It and Flip It technique, page 8,
sew the 1 1/4" x 1 1/4" white background squares to the sides
of the flowers, **Fig 5**; press.

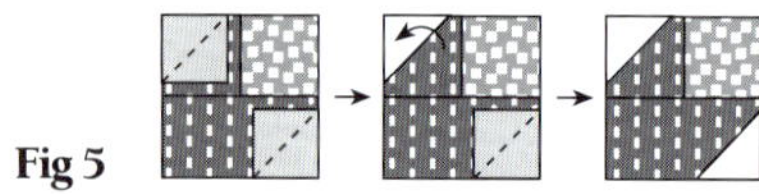

Fig 5

5. Strip piece the light background strips onto the top two
sides of the flowers, **Fig 6**; press.

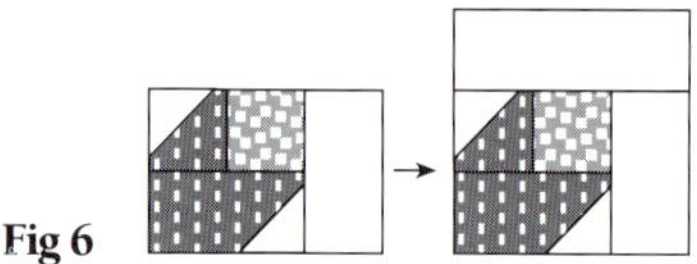

Fig 6

6. Strip piece med teal strips to the flower units; then strip
piece to dk teal strips, **Fig 7**. Press toward the outside of the
block after each addition.

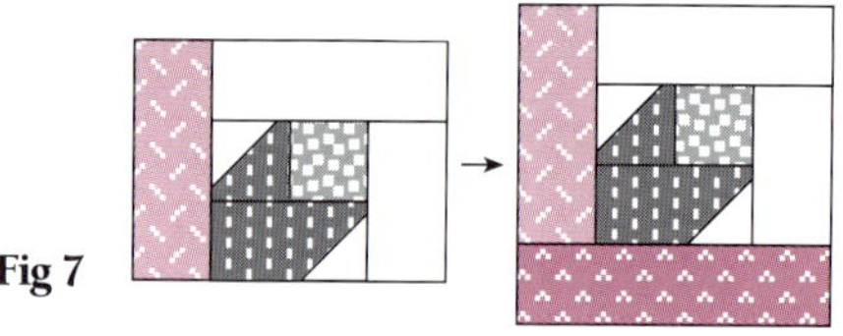

Fig 7

7. Using the Stitch It, Snip It and Flip It technique, page 8,
add the 2" x 2" squares to the ends of the leaves, **Fig 8**.
Repeat for all 24 Flower Blocks. Press.

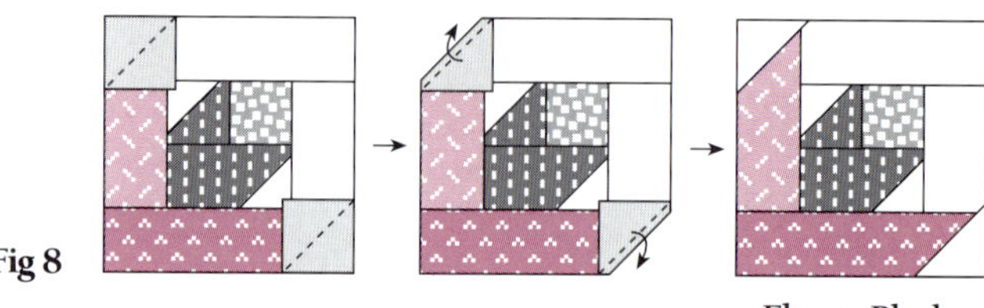

Fig 8

Flower Block

Making Large Blocks A and B

1. Square the Flower Blocks if necessary. They should measure 6 1/2" x 6 1/2" before assembly. Set aside four Blocks.

2. Piece together four Flower Blocks to create large Block A,
Fig 9; press. Repeat three more times.

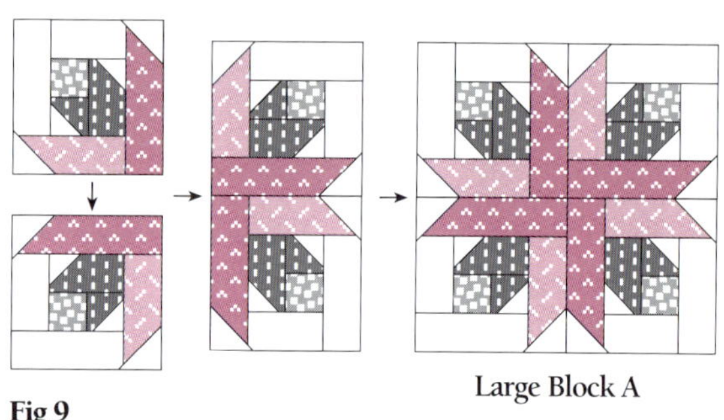

Fig 9

Large Block A

3. Piece together four Flower Blocks to complete one Large
Block B, **Fig 10**. Press.

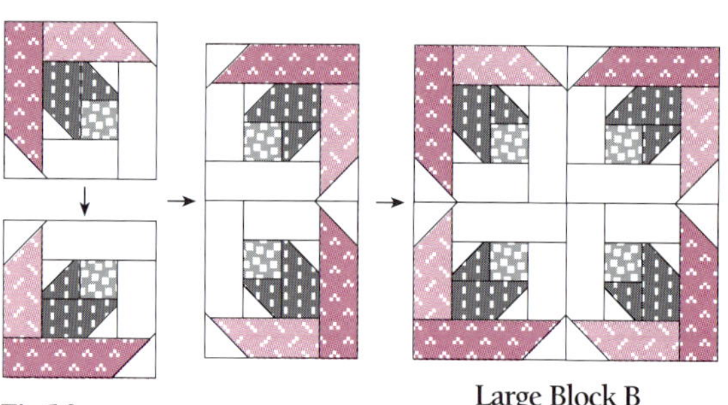

Fig 10

Large Block B

Making the Pieced Finishing Triangles

For Pieced Finishing Triangle, sew a floral finishing triangle
to each side of the top of one of the reserved Flower Blocks,
Fig 11. Make four.

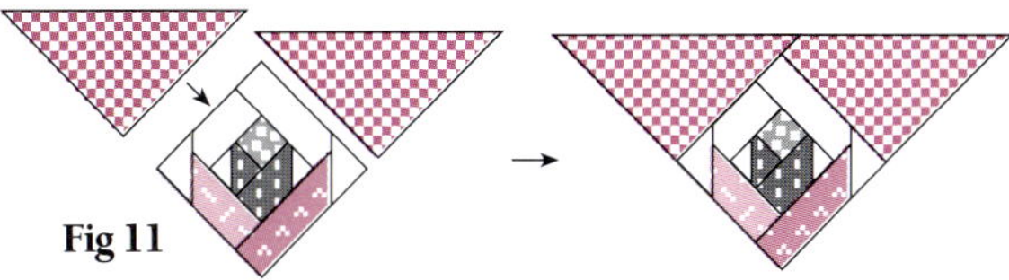

Fig 11

Assembling the Quilt

1. Place blocks and triangles in diagonal rows, **Fig 12**.

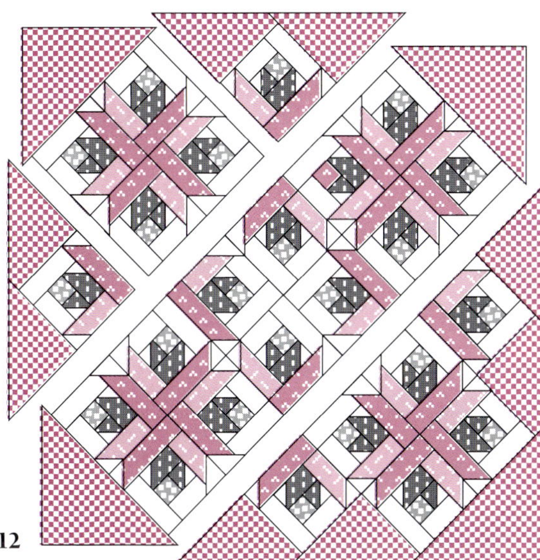

Fig 12

2. Sew borders to quilt according to Simple Borders, page 9.

3. See the General Directions, pages 9 to 11, for finishing
the quilt.

Make Mine Pansies

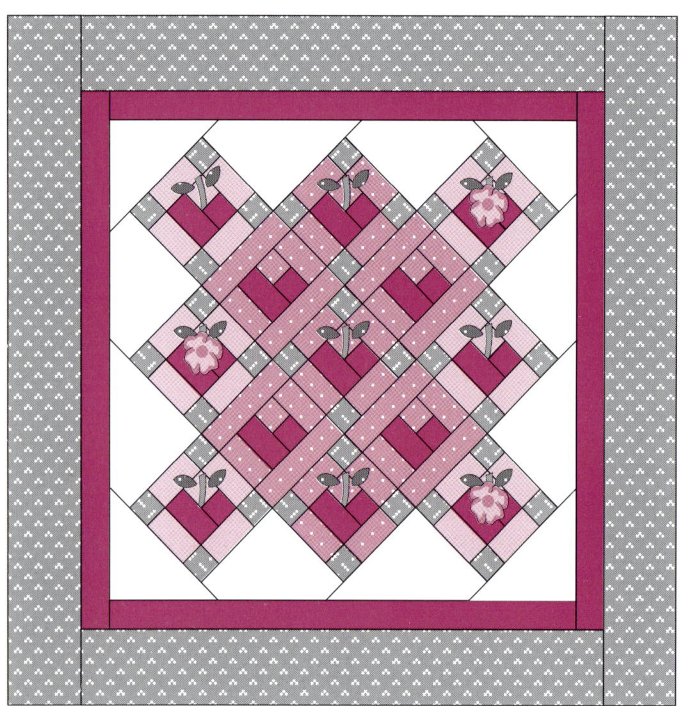

Shown in full color on front and back cover.

COLOR KEY

- Red Violet
- Check
- Yellow
- Gold
- Green
- Lt Tan
- Pansy Floral

APPROXIMATE SIZE: 39" X 39"

FINISHED BLOCK SIZE: 6" X 6"

The diagonal setting is perfect for the easy to cut and sew Heart and Pansy Pot Blocks. The different background fabrics in the blocks add extra sparkle to the design without extra effort. A touch of simple appliqué tops off the design.

Fabric Requirements:

1/3 yd red violet for hearts and first border
1/8 yd check for corners
1/4 yd yellow for background
1/3 yd gold for background
scraps of green prints for Stems and Leaves
1/2 yd lt tan for finishing and corner triangles
3/4 yd pansy floral for second border and binding
1 1/4 yds backing
1 1/4 yds batting

Note: *Three pansies and five leaves were taken from the pansy floral scraps and added to the wall hanging using paper-backed fusible web.*

Pattern Pieces (page 38):

Stem
Leaf

Cutting Requirements:

two 2"-wide" strips, red violet (hearts)
two 2" x 25" strips, check (corners)
two 2" x 15" strips, check (corners)
one 2" x 13" strip, yellow (background)
one 3 1/2" x 25" strip, yellow (background)
two 2" x 44" strips, gold (background)
one 3 1/2" x 15" strip, gold (background)
nine Stems, green prints
fifteen Leaves, green prints
two 10 1/2" x 10 1/2" squares, lt tan (cut in quarters diagonally for finishing triangles, **Fig 1**)
two 7" x 7" squares, lt tan (cut in half diagonally for corner triangles, **Fig 2**)

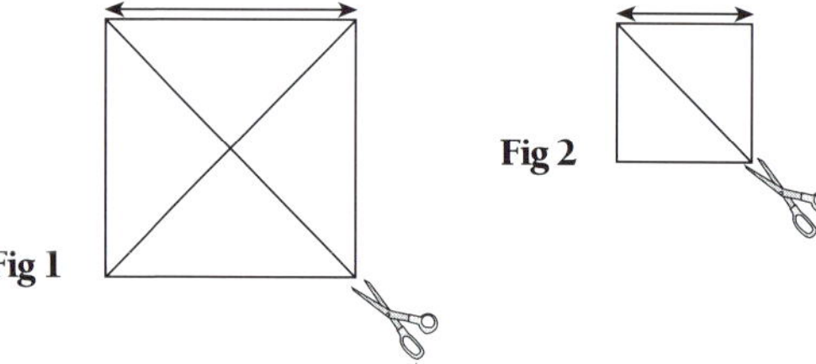

four 1 3/4 "-wide strips, red violet (first border)
four 4 1/2"-wide strips, pansy floral (second border)
four 2"-wide strips, pansy floral (binding)

Instructions:

Making Block A

1. Sew 2" x 15" gold strip to 2"-wide red violet strip, **Fig 3**; press to dark side. Cut sewn strips into seven 2"-wide units, **Fig 4**.

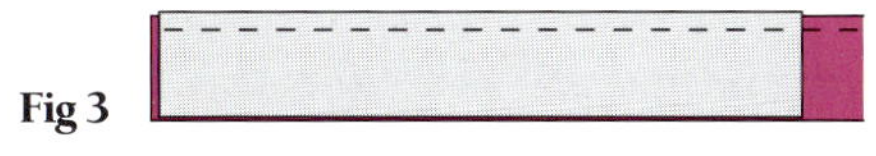

Fig 3

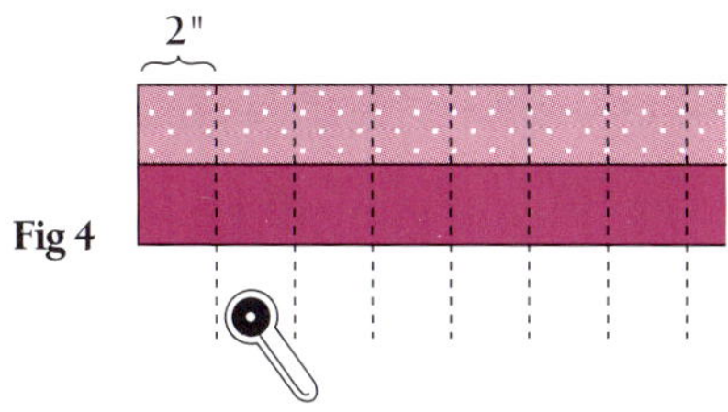

Fig 4

2. Strip piece unit to 2"-wide red violet strip; cut apart and press open for heart center, **Fig 5**.

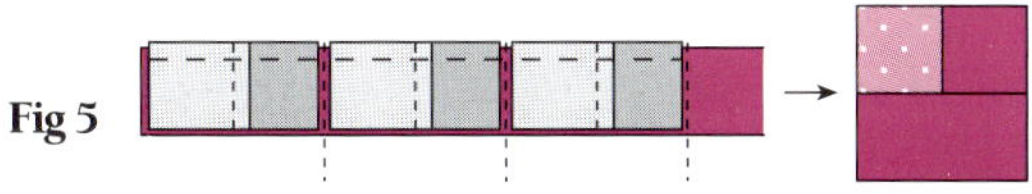

Fig 5

3. Sew 2"-wide gold strip to opposite sides of heart center; sew gold strip to remaining sides, **Fig 6**. Repeat for a total of four Block A.

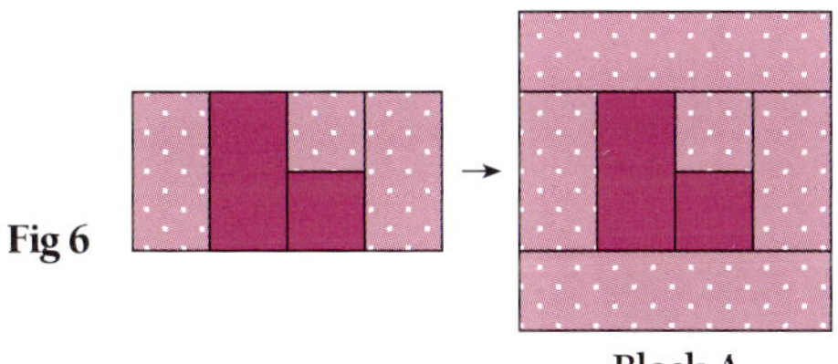

Fig 6

Block A

Making Block B

1. Stitch remaining three heart centers to 2"-wide gold strip, **Fig 7**; cut apart, then stitch gold strip to opposite side of heart center, **Fig 8**. Cut apart and press.

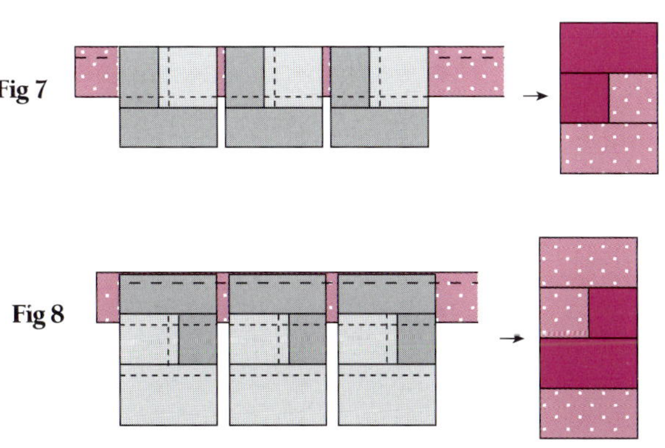

Fig 7

Fig 8

2. Sew two 2"-wide x 15" plaid strips to 3 1/2" x 15" gold strip; press to dark sides. Cut into six 2"-wide units, **Fig 9**.

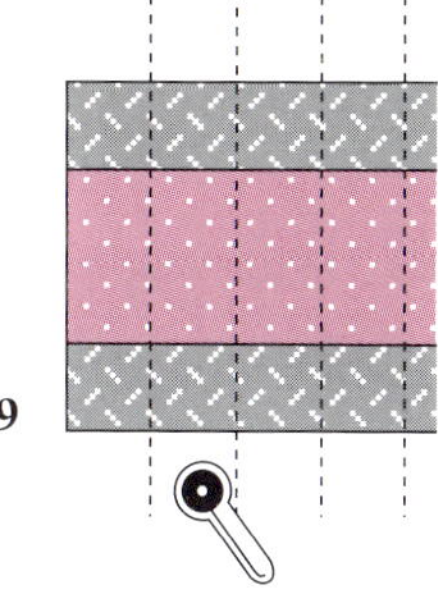

Fig 9

3. Sew units to remaining sides of heart center to complete Block B, **Fig 10**; press. Repeat for a total of three Block B.

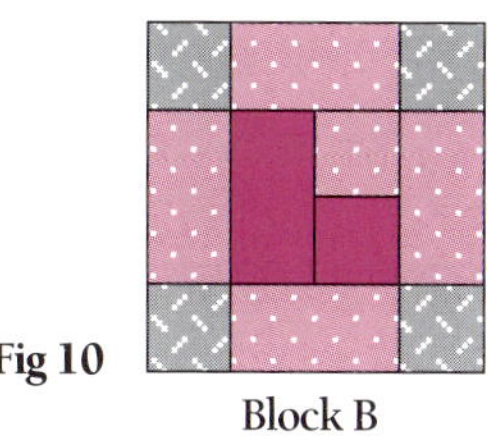

Fig 10

Block B

Making Block C

1. Sew 2" x 13" yellow strip to 2"-wide red violet strip, **Fig 11**; press to dark side. Cut into six 2"-wide units, **Fig 12**.

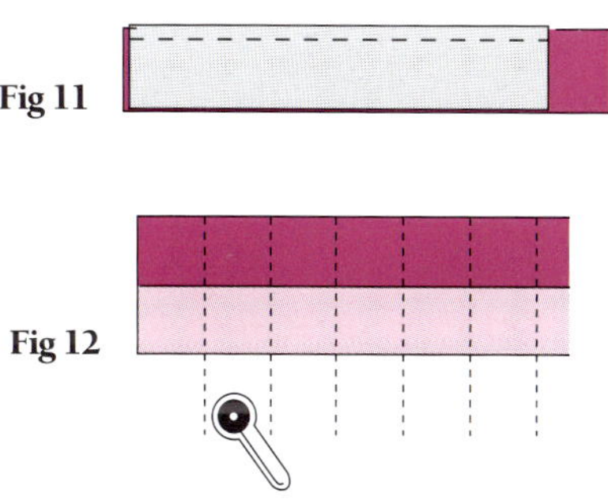

Fig 11

Fig 12

2. Strip piece unit to 2"-wide red violet strip; cut apart and press open, **Fig 13**. Sew 2"-wide yellow strip to opposite sides, **Fig 14**.

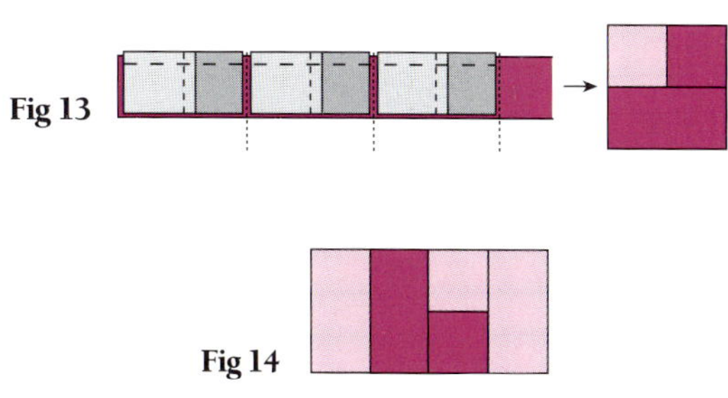

Fig 13

Fig 14

continued

3. Sew a 2" x 25" plaid strip to each long side of 3 1/2" x 25" yellow strip; press to dark side. Cut into twelve 2"-wide units, **Fig 15**.

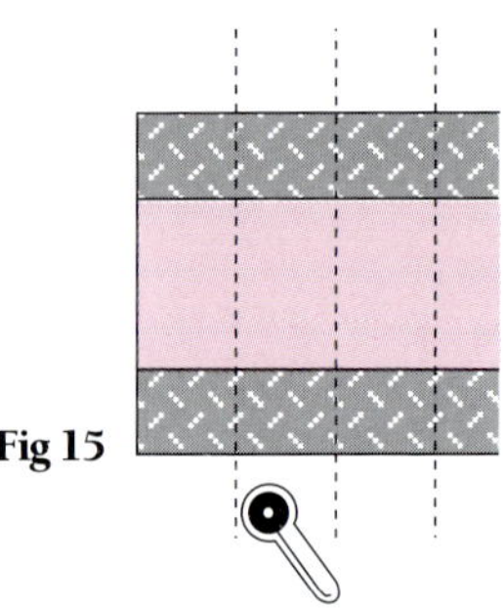

Fig 15

4. Sew units to opposite sides to complete Block C, **Fig 16**. Repeat for a total of six Block C.

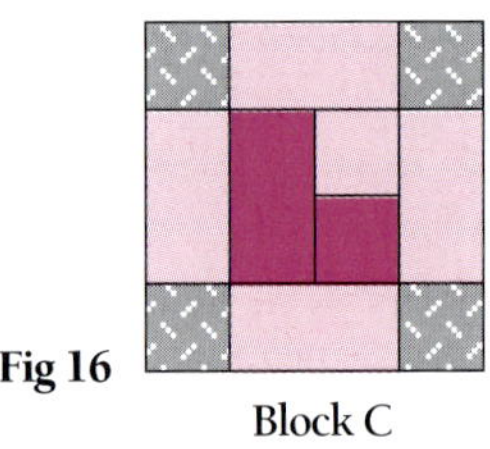

Fig 16

Block C

Assembling the Quilt

1. Place Tulips Blocks A, B and C, finishing triangles and corner triangles as in **Fig 17**. Sew together in diagonal rows; then sew rows together.

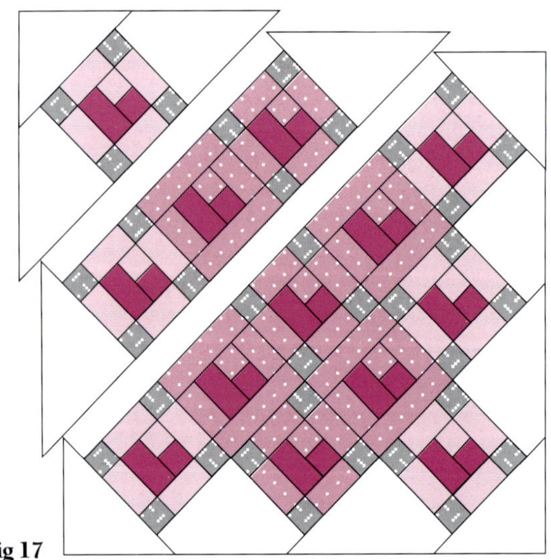

Fig 17

Note: *To create the illusion that the blocks are floating on the background, all of the finishing triangles and corners are oversized.*

2. Sew borders to quilt according to Simple Borders, page 9.

3. Appliqué nine Stems and fifteen Leaves referring to Basic Hand and Machine Appliqué, page 8.

4. Referring to manufacturer's directions, fuse paper-backed fusible web to wrong side of pansy floral fabric; cut out. (Photographed quilt has three pansies and five leaves from pansy floral fabric.) Fuse to quilt following manufacturer's directions.

5. See the General Directions, pages 9 to 11, for finishing the quilt.

Pattern Pieces

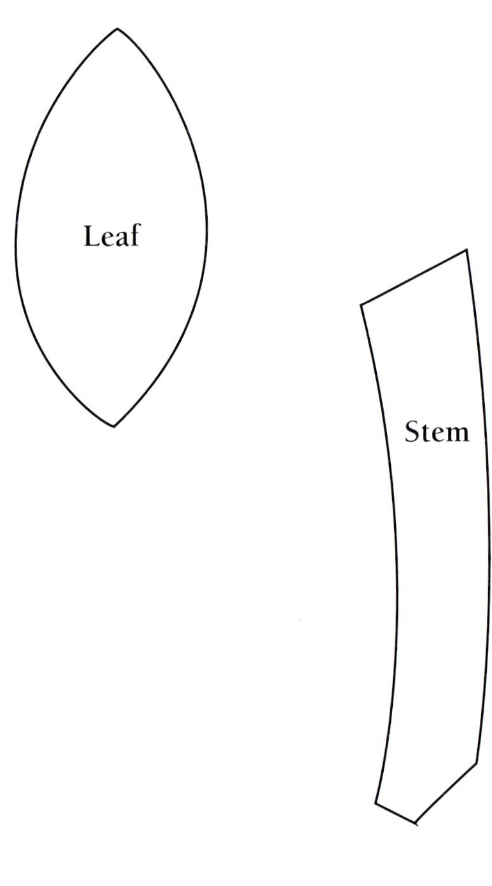

Flowering Garden

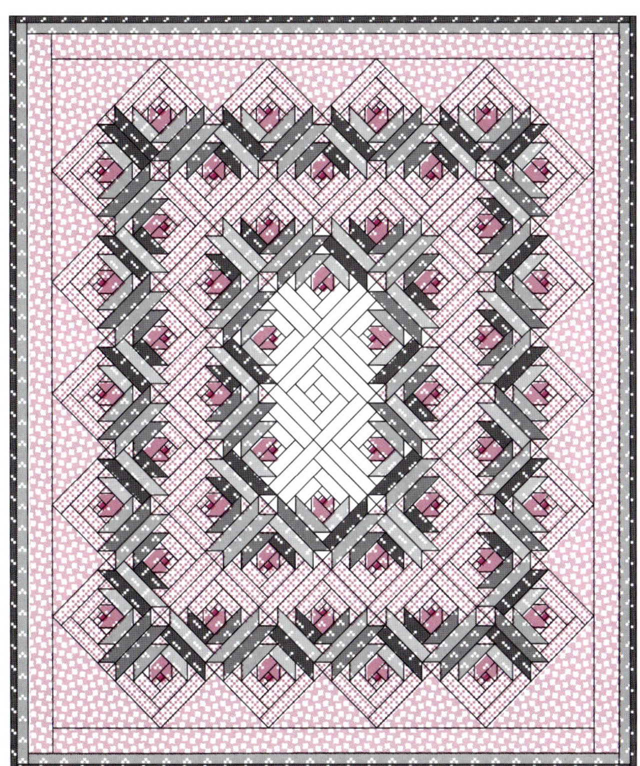

Shown in full color on page 24.

COLOR KEY

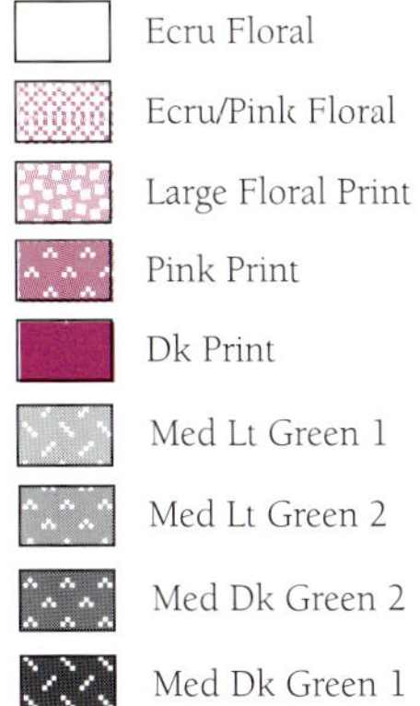

APPROXIMATE SIZE: 94" x 110" (to fit full/queen bed)

FINISHED BLOCK SIZE: 12" x 12" SQUARE

Remarkably, this large quilt has only 49 twelve-inch blocks. The three different background fabrics add interest and appeal to the formal diagonal setting.

Fabric Requirements:

3/4 yd ecru floral (Fabric A) for background of center blocks

3 1/2 yds ecru/pink floral (Fabric B) for background of 42 blocks

3 1/4 yds large floral print (Fabric C) for finishing triangles and first border

1 yd total pink prints (if using scraps allow 2 1/2" x 9" per tulip) for tulips

1/8 yd dark print for centers of tulips

1 yd each of four green print fabrics (choose two med lt and two med dk) for leaves

3/4 yd med lt green print for second border

3/4 yd med dk green print for binding

8 1/2 yds 44"-wide fabric or 3 1/2 yds 109"-wide fabric for backing

120" x 120" batting

Cutting Requirements:

Note: *Cut strips on crosswise grain.*

one 1 1/2"-wide strip, Fabric A (background)

four 1 1/2"-wide strips, Fabric B (background)

six 2 1/2"-wide strips, Fabric A (background)

twelve 2" x 2" squares, Fabric A (background)

29 - 2 1/2"-wide strips, Fabric B (background)

84 - 2" x 2" squares, Fabric B (background)

eleven 2 1/2"-wide strips, pink print (tulips)

two 1 1/2"-wide strips, dk print (centers)

twelve 2 1/2"-wide strips of fabric from each of four green print fabrics (leaves)

36 - 2 1/2" x 2 1/2" squares, Fabric A (background)

252 - 2 1/2" x 2 1/2" squares, Fabric B (background)

four 18 1/2" x 18 1/2" squares, Fabric C (cut diagonally into quarters for finishing triangles)

two 17 1/2" x 17 1/2" squares, Fabric C (cut in half diagonally for corner triangles)

nine 4"-wide strips, Fabric C (first border)

ten 1 3/4"-wide strips, med lt green print (second border)

ten 2 1/4"-wide strips, med dk green print (binding)

continued

Instructions:

Tulip Block A

1. Sew together 1 1/2"-wide dk print strip and 1 1/2"-wide Fabric A strip. Press to dk fabric and cut into six 1 1/2"-wide units, **Fig 1**.

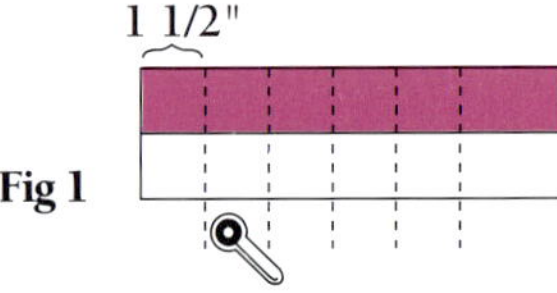

Fig 1

2. Strip piece the 1 1/2"-wide units to 1 1/2"-wide fabric A strips, **Fig 2**.

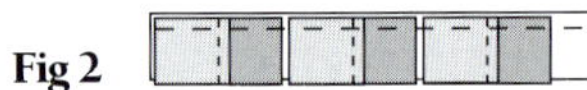

Fig 2

3. Cut apart; open and finger press, **Fig 3**.

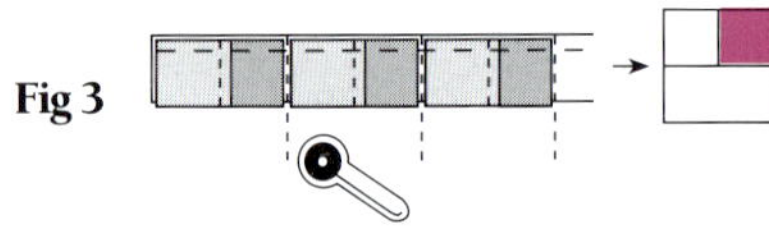

Fig 3

4. Strip these centers to 2 1/2"-wide pink print strips; cut apart. Open and finger press, **Fig 4**.

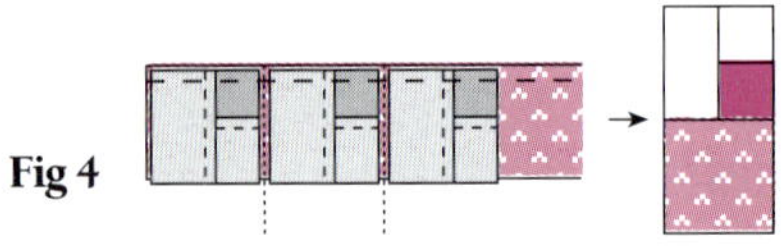

Fig 4

5. Finish the tulip by strip piecing the unit to 2 1/2"-wide pink print strips. Cut apart; open and press, **Fig 5**.

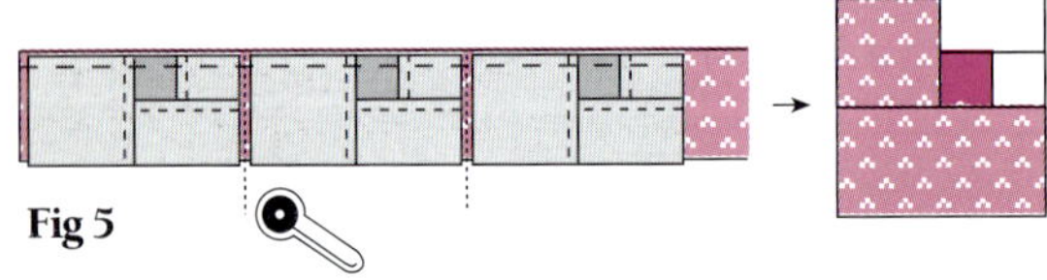

Fig 5

6. Sew the 2" background squares to the corners of the flower using the Stitch It, Flip It and Snip It technique, page 8, **Fig 6**.

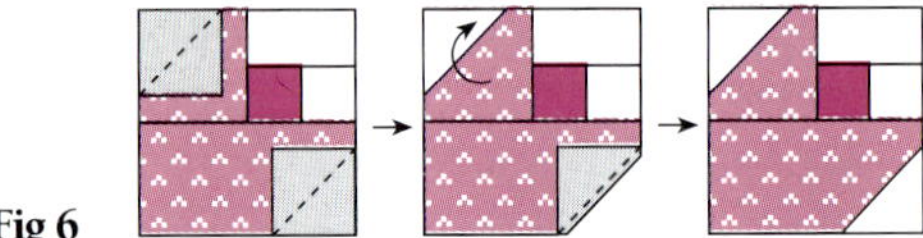

Fig 6

7. Strip piece 2 1/2"-wide fabric A background strips to top two sides of tulip, **Fig 7**.

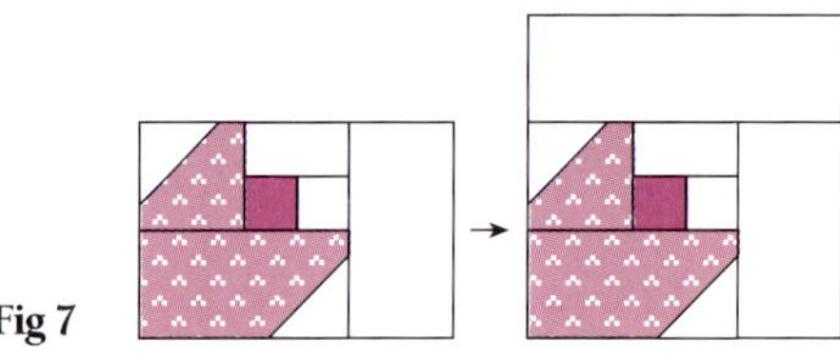

Fig 7

8. Strip piece the med lt green print leaves to lower sides of tulip units, **Fig 8**.

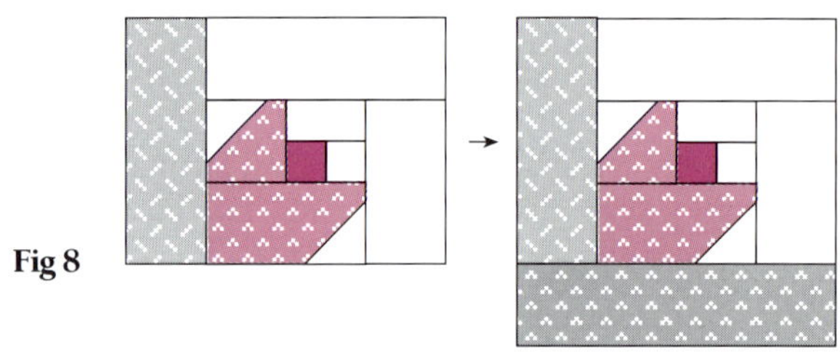

Fig 8

9. Using the Stitch It, Snip It and Flip It technique, page 8, sew three 2 1/2" background squares to the corners of the leaves, **Fig 9**.

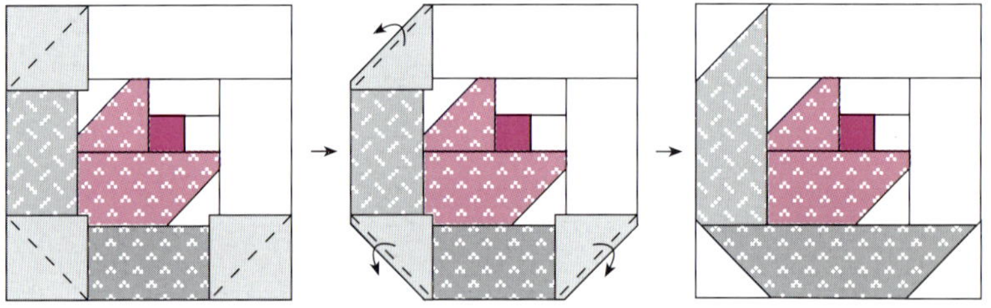

Fig 9

10. Strip piece 2 1/2"-wide fabric A background strips to top two sides of tulip, **Fig 10**.

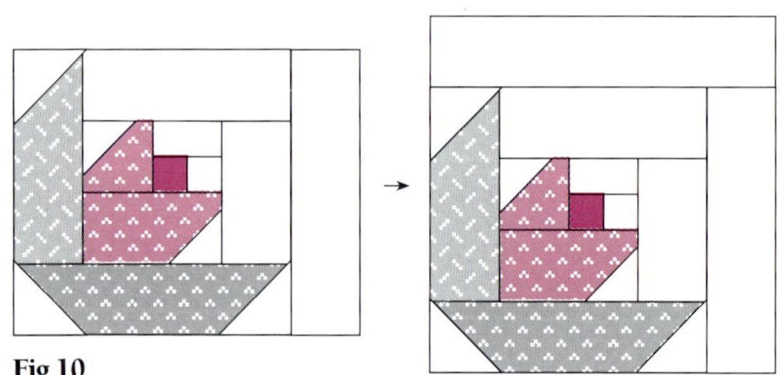

Fig 10

11. Strip piece med dk green 2 1/2"-wide leaf strips to bottom two sides of tulip, **Fig 11**.

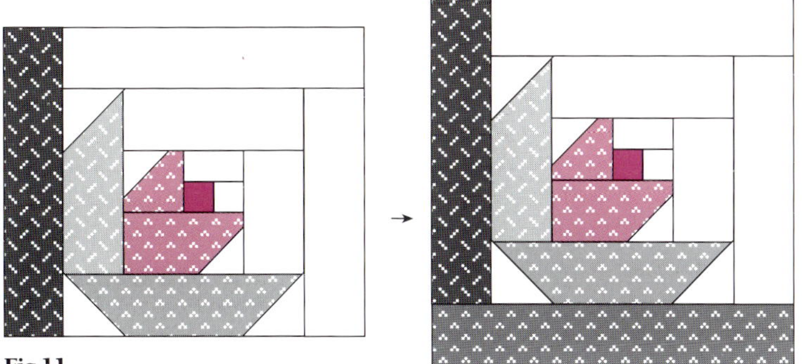

Fig 11

Log Cabin Block

Make one Log Cabin Block for the very center of the quilt referring to Log Cabin, page 8; use 2 1/2"-wide strips from background Fabric A, **Fig 15**.

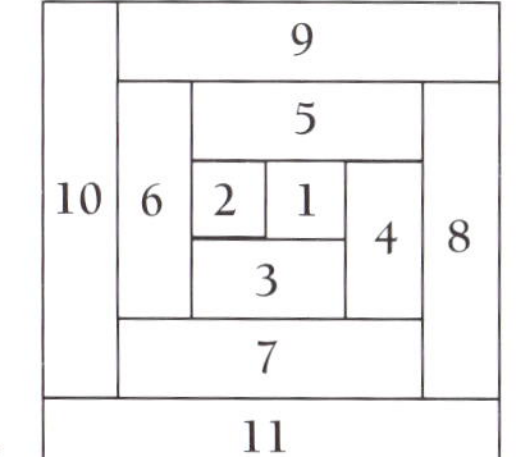

Fig 15

12. Using Stitch It, Snip It and Flip It technique, sew 2 1/2"-wide fabric A squares onto corners of leaves, **Fig 12**; press. Make a total of six Tulip Block A.

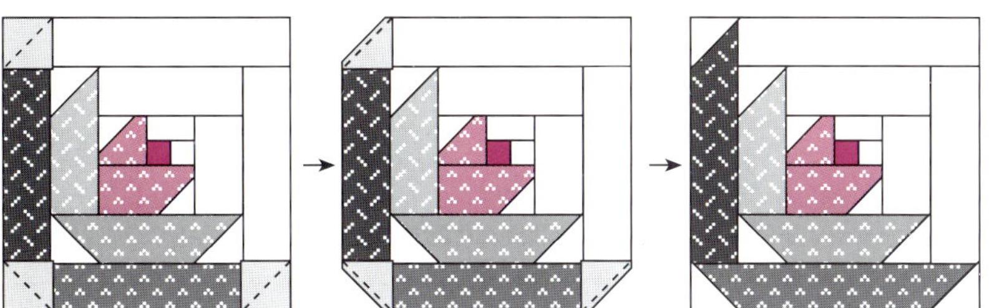

Fig 12

Tulip Block A

Assembling the Quilt

1. Place Tulip Blocks, finishing triangles and corner triangles following quilt layout below. Note that blocks are placed according to the placement of the background fabrics, A, B and C.

2. Sew the borders onto the quilt according to Simple Borders, page 9.

3. Refer to General Directions, pages 9 to 11, for finishing the quilt.

Tulip Block B1

For Tulip Block B1, repeat steps 1 to 12 of Tulip Block A to complete 18 Tulip Block B1, **Fig 13**; use ecru/pink floral background fabric.

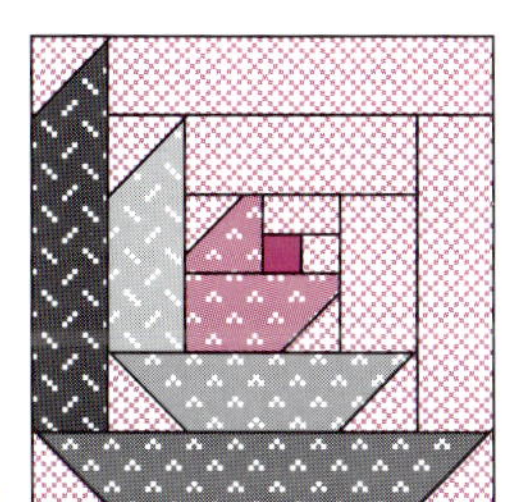

Fig 13

Tulip Block B1

Tulip Block B2

For Tulip Block B2, repeat steps 1 to 12 of Tulip Block A to complete 24 Tulip Block B2, **Fig 14**; use ecru/pink floral background fabric and add med dk green print strips before adding med lt green.

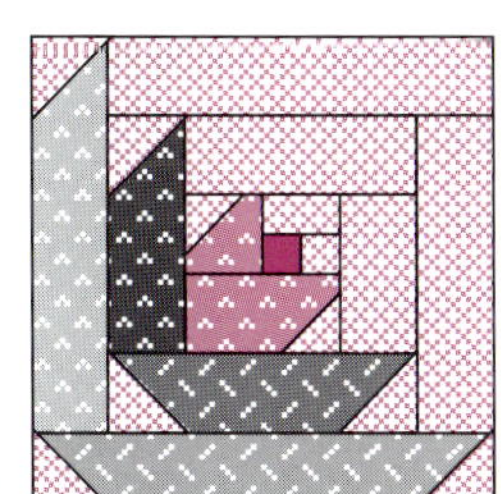

Fig 14

Tulip Block B2

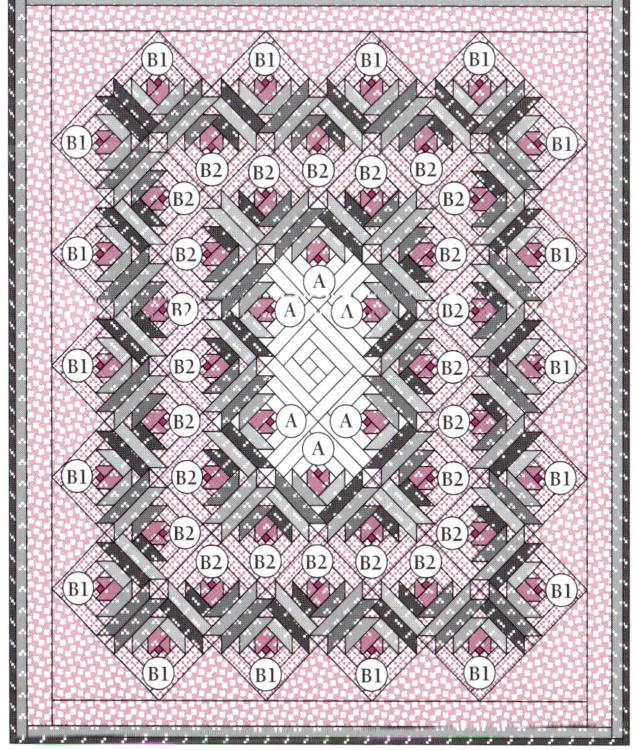

Quilt Layout

It's the Berries

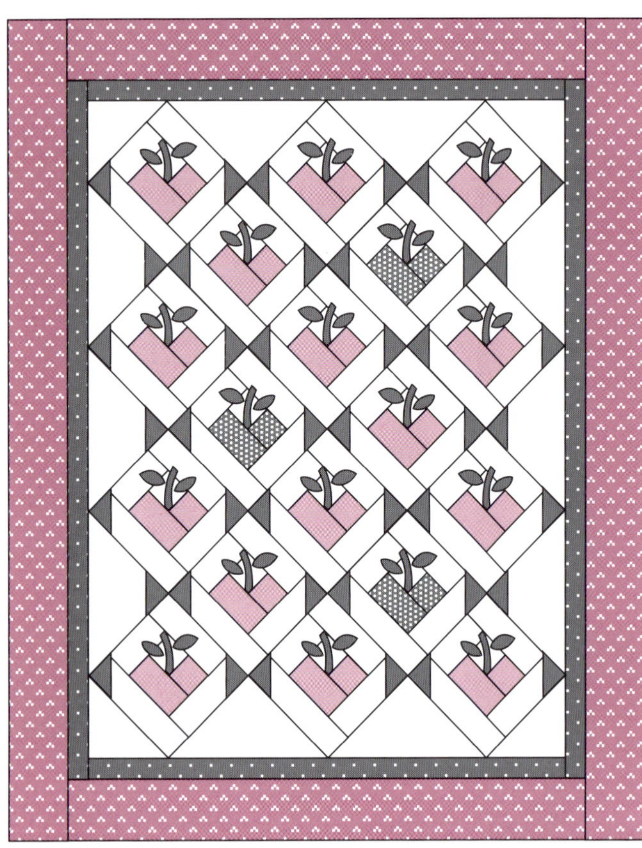

Shown in full color on page 23.

COLOR KEY

☐	White
☐	Blue Print
☐	Red Print
☐	Green Pin Dot
☐	Red Border Print
☐	Blue Border Print

APPROXIMATE SIZE: 47" x 58"

FINISHED BLOCK SIZE: 8" x 8"

You'll want to relax under this comfortable machine-pieced and appliquéd quilt with a hot cup of tea and a good book. Machine tacking joins the top, bottom and extra thick polyester batting. Make it today to enjoy tomorrow.

Fabric Requirements:

2 yds white for background
1/4 yd blue print for berries
1/8 yd red print for berries
3/8 yd green pin dot for stems and leaves
1/4 yd red print for first border
1 yd blue print for second border
2 1/2 yds backing
twin batting

Pattern Pieces (page 44):

Stem
Leaf

Cutting Requirements:

twelve 2 1/2"-wide strips, white (background)
three 2 1/2"-wide strips, blue print (berries)
one 2 1/2"-wide strip, red print (berries)
42 - 2 1/2" x 2 1/2" squares, green pin dot
three 13" x 13" squares, white (cut diagonally into
    quarters for finishing triangles, **Fig 1**)
two 7" x 7" squares, white (cut in half diagonally for
    corner triangles, **Fig 2**)

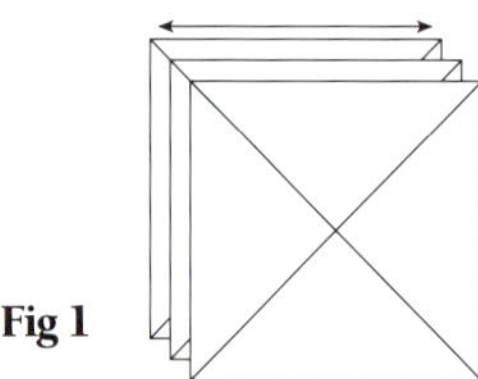

Fig 1

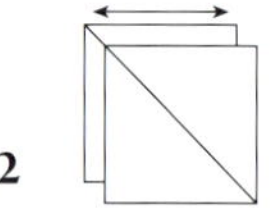

Fig 2

six 1 1/2"-wide strips, red (first border)
six 6"-wide strips, blue print (second border)
*36 Leaves, green pin dot
*18 Stems, green pin dot
*Read Basic Hand and Machine Appliqué, Easy Machine
Technique, page 8, before cutting Stems and Leaves from fabric.

Instructions:

Making the Berry Block

1. Sew together one 2 1/2"-wide
blue print strip with one 2 1/2"-
wide background strip; press
toward darker fabric. Cut at 2 1/2"
intervals, **Fig 3**.

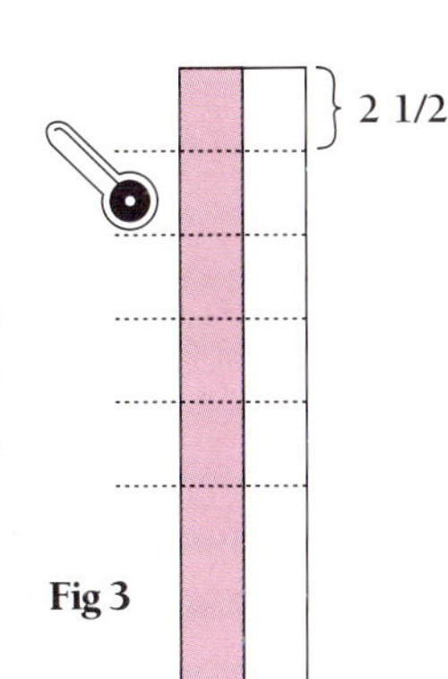

2. Cut a 2 1/2"-wide red print and a 2 1/2"-wide background
strip into 9" lengths; sew together. Cut into three 2 1/2"
units, **Fig 4**.

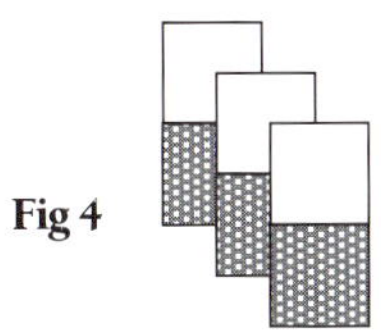

3. Strip piece the units onto the matching print strips, **Fig 5**.

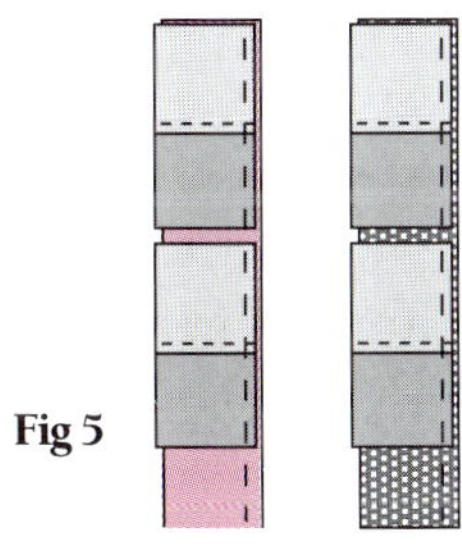

4. Cut apart and finger press open, **Fig 6**.

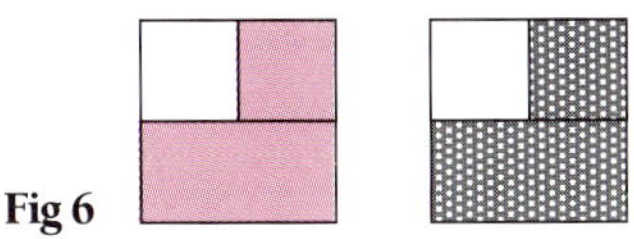

5. Chain stitch background strips onto the sides of the heart
center, **Fig 7**. See General Directions for Log Cabin
Technique, page 8. Make 18 blocks.

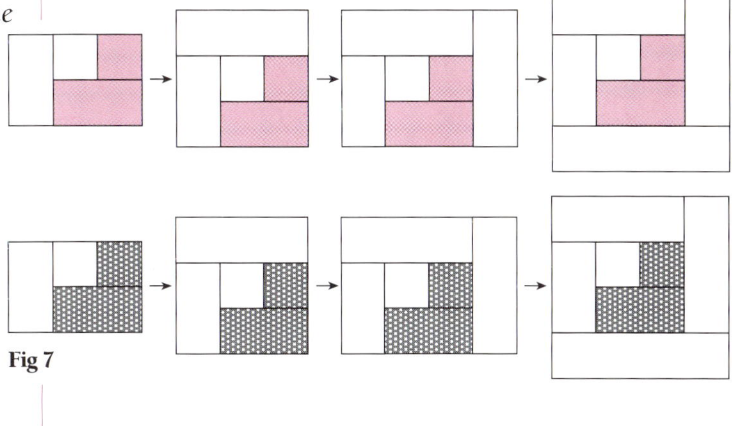

6. Press all seams toward outside of block.

7. Sew 2 1/2" green pin dot corners to all blocks using the
Stitch It, Snip It and Flip It technique (see page 8), **Fig 8**.
Refer to Basic Hand and Machine Appliqué, page 8, to add
Stems and Leaves to each Berry Block, **Fig 9**.

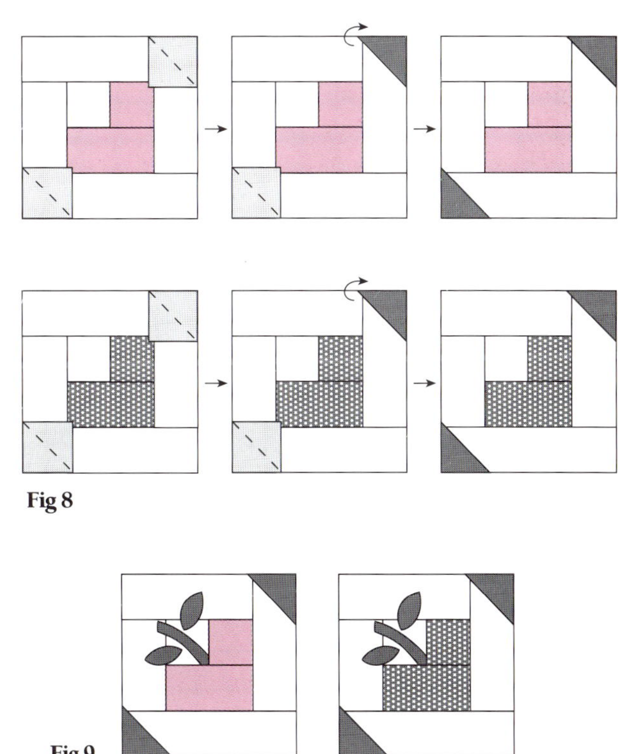

continued

8. Sew the remaining 2 1/2" green pin dot squares to six of the finishing triangles, **Fig 10**; use the Stitch It, Snip It and Flip It technique.

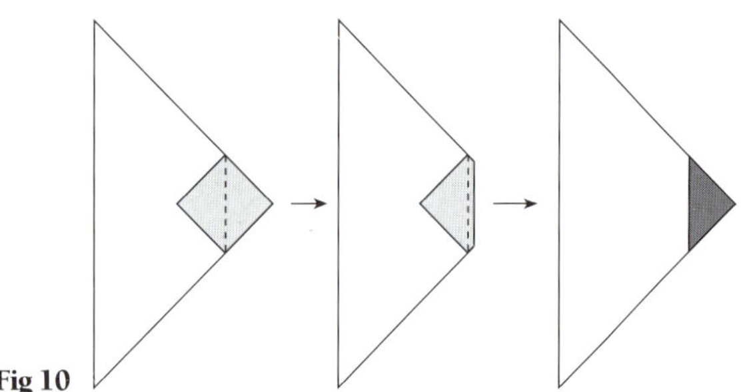

Fig 10

Assembling the Quilt

1. Place Berry Blocks, finishing triangles and corner triangles in diagonal rows, **Fig 11**; sew together in rows, then sew rows together.

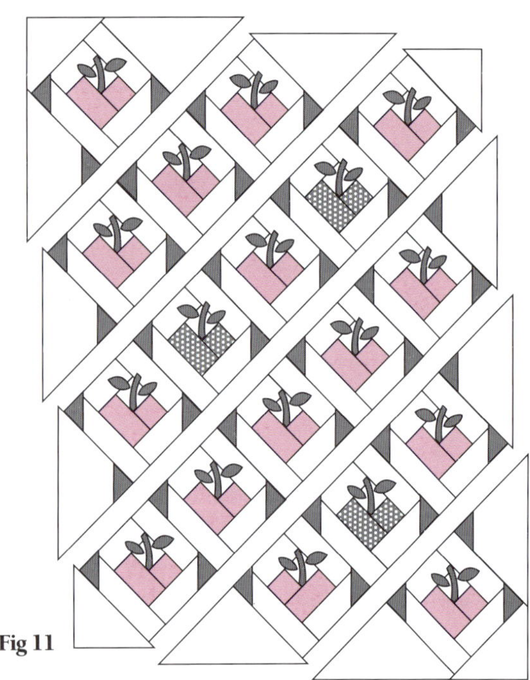

Fig 11

2. Sew the borders to quilt referring to Simple Borders, page 9.

3. Refer to General Directions, pages 9 to 11, to finish the quilt. Photographed quilt was machine tacked at corners of berries and Berry Blocks.

Pattern Pieces

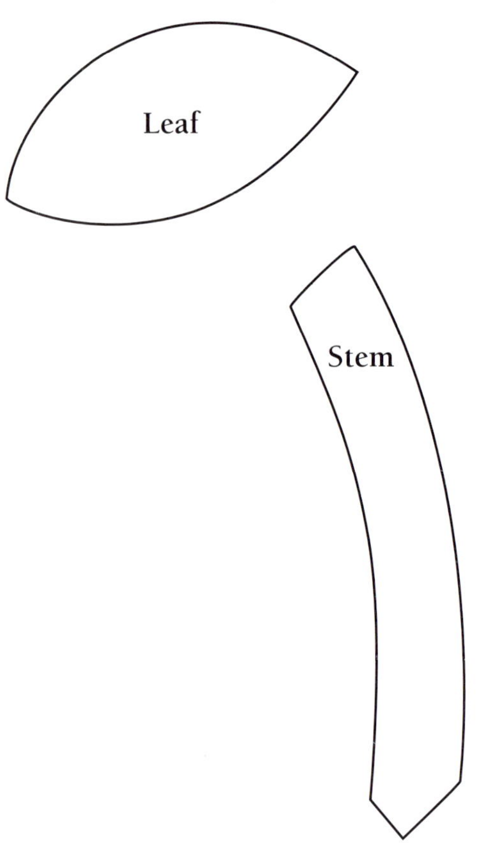